Home Repairs Bible

The complete guide with Step-by-Step Projects, Expert Tips, and Money-Saving Strategies for Remodeling, Renovating, and Maintaining Your Home

BOB L. CARTER

BOB L. CARTER © Copyright 2023 - All rights reserved.

The content contained within this book may not be reproduced, duplicated or transmitted without direct written permission from the author or the publisher.

Under no circumstances will any blame or legal responsibility be held against the publisher, or author, for any damages, reparation, or monetary loss due to the information contained within this book. Either directly or indirectly.

Legal Notice:

This book is copyright protected. This book is only for personal use. You cannot amend, distribute, sell, use, quote or paraphrase any part, or the content within this book, without the consent of the author or publisher.

Disclaimer Notice:

Please note the information contained within this document is for educational and entertainment purposes only. All effort has been executed to present accurate, up to date, and reliable, complete information. No warranties of any kind are declared or implied. Readers acknowledge that the author is not engaging in the rendering of legal, financial, medical or professional advice. The content within this book has been derived from various sources. Please consult a licensed professional before attempting any techniques outlined in this book.

By reading this document, the reader agrees that under no circumstances is the author responsible for any losses, direct or indirect, which are incurred as a result of the use of information contained within this document, including, but not limited to, — errors, omissions, or inaccuracies.

TABLE OF CONTENTS

THANK YOU!! 9

DOWNLOAD YOUR SPECIAL BONUS GUIDE 10

INTRODUCTION 11

PART 1: SAFETY FIRST 12

Safety equipment 12

PPE, or personal protective equipment 12

Easy and safe DIY: clothing 13

Work gloves for DIY 14

The safety shoes 15

DIY jobs: hearing protection 15

Do it yourself home repairs: construction helmet 16

Dust masks for DIY 17

Safety goggles 18

Hand wash 18

Fire extinguisher 19

Basic safety procedures 19

Electrical safety 20

Ladder safety 22

Working with power tools 23

Working with hazardous materials 23

PART 2: TOOLS AND MATERIALS 25

Essential tools for home repairs and improvement 25

The toolbox 26

Screwdriver set 27

Some pliers, the most versatile tool 28

English keys 29

Rollable measuring tape 29

- Drill 29
- The ladder 29
- Level 29
- Clothing 30
- Hammer 30
- Lamp with hook 31

Types of fasteners and hardware 31
- Hardware types 31
- Fastener types 32

Types of adhesives and sealants 33
- The adhesives types 34
- The sealants types 35
- Features to consider when choosing 35

Choosing the right paint and finishes 36
- What type of paint to choose for improving your home? 37
- Finishes choice 37

PART 3: PLUMBING 40
Basic plumbing repairs 40
- The materials used and the types 41
- Types of plumbing 42

Replacing faucets and fixtures 43
- How to change a do-it-yourself faucet? 43
- How to replace the fixtures 45

Fixing leaks and clogs 46
- How to fix leaky faucet 46
- How to fix clogs 47

Installing a new toilet or sink 48
- Installing a new toilet 48
- Installing a new sink 52

Upgrading your water heater 54
Step-by-step projects 55

1. Replace a leaky faucet 55
2. Fix a running toilet 55
3. Install a new showerhead 56
4. Replace a toilet flange 57
5. Fix a clogged sink 59
6. Replace a damaged pipe 59
7. Install a new water filtration system 60
8. Add a new outdoor faucet 61
9. Replace a bathtub drain 63
10. Install a new garbage disposal 63

PART 4: ELECTRICAL 65

Basic electrical repairs 65

Secure electrical connections 65

Water repellent protection 66

Clogged hose 66

Conductor interrupted 66

Prepare the ends of the electrical wires 66

Tin the lugs 66

Repair circuit boards 67

Use the phase finder 67

Does the earth work? 67

Calibrate the tester 67

Replacing outlets and switches 67

Replacing electrical outlets: the phases of the work 68

Replace switches 69

Wiring a new circuit or outlet 71
Installing lighting fixtures and ceiling fans 72

Ceiling fan: how to install it 73

Upgrading your electrical panel 76
Step-by-step electrician projects 76

1. Replace a light switch 77
2. Install a ceiling fan 77
3. Replace a light fixture 77
4. Replace a circuit breaker 78
5. Install a new smoke detector 78
6. Install a new doorbell 79

PART 5: Heating, Ventilation, and Air Conditioning (HVAC) 80
Basic HVAC maintenance and repairs 80
Replacing filters and thermostats 81
Installing a new HVAC system: a step-by-step project 83
Replace an air filter 83
Clean the air ducts 83
Install a programmable thermostat 84
Install a new air conditioner 85
Install a humidifier or dehumidifier 89
Install a ductless mini-split system 90
Add a smart thermostat and control system 91

Upgrading your insulation and weatherization 92
Insulation 92
Weatherization 92

PART 6: Carpentry and Woodworking 94
Basic carpentry skills 94
Repairing or replacing damaged trim and molding 98
Building custom shelves and cabinets 99
Installing hardwood floors or laminate flooring 101
Installing Hardwood Floors 101
Installing Laminate Flooring 102

step-by-step projects 103
1. Build a custom bookshelf 103
2. Build a window seat or bench 104
Build a floating shelf 105

  3. Build a wooden headboard 106

  4. Build a birdhouse or bird feeder 107

 Build a birdhouse 108

 Build a bird feeder 109

  5. Build a simple table or desk 110

PART 7: PAINTING AND DECORATING 112

Choosing the right paint and finishes 112
Painting techniques and tips 112
Repairing and preparing walls for painting 113
Installing wallpaper or wall coverings 115
A painting step-by-step project 116

 Refinish a piece of furniture 116

 Install crown molding 117

 Paint or stain kitchen cabinets 118

 Paint or stain a front door 119

 Install a statement light fixture 120

 Add decorative tile to a backsplash or fireplace 121

PART 8: OUTDOOR IMPROVEMENTS 123

Landscaping and garden design 123
Installing a new patio or deck 124
Adding a pool or hot tub 125
Repairing or replacing your roof 126
Outdoor improvement step-by-step projects 127

 Build a raised garden bed 127

 Install a patio or deck 130

 Build an outdoor kitchen or grill station 131

 Install a water feature or fountain 132

 Install a pergola or gazebo 133

 Build a treehouse or playset 134

PART 9: RENOVATIONS 136

Kitchen remodeling 136

- **Bathroom remodeling** 137
- **Basement finishing** 137
- **Adding an addition to your home** 138

CHAPTER 10: HOME MAINTENANCE 140

- **Regular home maintenance tasks** 140
- **Seasonal home maintenance tasks** 141
  - Monthly 141
  - Seasonal 141
- **Creating home maintenance schedule** 142
- **Hiring professionals for maintenance and repairs** 144

THANK YOU!!

Take a photo or video of your book, and tell everyone what do you think about it!

Scan the QR CODE, upload the photo/video and you're done!

Your feedback is essential to improve the quality of my books; the opinions of my readers are lifeblood to me, and I really appreciate every comments.

Thank you very much in advance.

DOWNLOAD YOUR SPECIAL BONUS GUIDE

Discover the exclusive bonus ready for you!

Scan the QR CODE to access the free bonus, you will receive it immediately ready to download!

A sample of the book "PLUMBING BIBLE". I'm sure you will like it.

Introduction

This is a complete book about "Home Repair and Improvement Bible".

The main purpose of this practical guide is to empower readers to take care of their homes and tackle a variety of repair and improvement projects on their own.

Where to start? Surely to give a new face to the house with a do-it-yourself renovation you need to have a great predisposition to manual skills and creativity, perhaps with an eye to recycling by reviving materials and objects that would end up in the dustbin.

If you are here, it is because you are interested in the idea of renovating your home with your own hands. We tell you that it is a very possible undertaking, you will meet your difficulties but for this reason it is not impossible to achieve. Renovations usually don't require high skills and knowledge and we are right here to help you.

By providing clear, step-by-step instructions and helpful tips and tricks, the book aims to give readers the knowledge and confidence they need to successfully complete projects and save money by avoiding the need for professional help.

In addition to practical goals like saving money and improving the functionality and appearance of their homes, the book also has the potential to improve readers' quality of life.

As soon as you finish reading this guide, we are sure that these objectives will certainly become yours and that you will be able to create a home environment of your dreams.

However, this guide will be divided into 10 chapters and each of them will address everything related to improving your home. Overall, the goal of the book is to provide readers with the knowledge, skills, and confidence they need to take control of their home repair and improvement projects and create a home that they can be proud of.

PART 1: Safety First

This chapter covers the most important safety guidelines that readers should follow while working on home improvement projects. Topics covered include proper tool use and handling, electrical safety, ladder safety, and working with hazardous materials such as paint and chemicals. The chapter also covers common accidents that can occur while working on home projects and how to prevent them. By following the safety guidelines outlined in this chapter, readers can ensure that they stay safe while working on their homes and avoid accidents and injuries.

Safety equipment

You don't know how to renovate the house or even just renovate it at its best? Do you have to evaluate how to transform an apartment you would like to buy or are you looking for new ideas to change the one you live in? When deciding to renovate, there are many aspects to consider: in addition to the choice of new materials, from parquet to tiles, from bathroom fixtures to taps for the bathroom and kitchen, up to the fixtures, there are numerous problems that also concern necessary bureaucracy, regulations and safety during the works.

Safety first: this is true in the workplace, if you practice a certain sport but, even more so, if you want to repair some elements of your home, the issue of safety becomes predominant. If you decide to renovate your home yourself, knowing who oversees the decisive safety could surprise you. If you are intent on renovating your home, you should know that you are solely and exclusively responsible for safety.

Either way, you'll need to have the proper tools and equipment when it comes to the safety of doing home repairs. Know that it is mandatory to have a good standard of tools that allow you to carry out all your repair and improvement work in a way that is not only effective but above all safe.

So, when buying, get only those that meet the established safety standards and are suitable for home use. Therefore, invest in quality equipment that is, at the same time, useful for your intended purpose. Renovating your home on your own could therefore be fun, but without forgetting to safeguard your own safety and security.

In fact, thinking that certain items of clothing are only necessary for professional work could be a serious error of assessment.

It should be remembered that domestic accidents, even when doing small jobs, are very frequent.

PPE, or personal protective equipment

Being passionate about DIY or simply want to do home repairs and improvement doesn't necessarily mean being an expert with all the tools of the trade.

In fact, there are those who, to the detriment of their own safety, do not take basic precautions to dispel any risk.

For this there are personal protective equipment which can be divided into:

- ✓ Clothing
- ✓ Gloves
- ✓ Shoes
- ✓ Work ear muffs
- ✓ Construction helmets
- ✓ Dust/gas masks
- ✓ Safety goggles
- ✓ Hand wash
- ✓ Extinguisher.

The rules for working in full safety are not very many and not even complicated. Precisely for this reason, however, they often tend to be forgotten.

For certain types of work, it would be good practice to also have a small fire extinguisher, as in the case of work involving electrical systems or welding.

Easy and safe DIY: clothing

Clothing must be appropriate. It is preferable to use full coveralls that cover the arms and legs without leaving parts of the body exposed, especially if the work to be done involves the production of dust or sawdust. Belts, buckles, necklaces and rings must be removed to work more easily and to prevent them from causing injury. Every DIY job has the most suitable dress to use for your own safety. For example, starting from welding work or when dealing with electrical material, there are suitable flame-retardant clothing.

These can be full protection, such as aprons made of cowhide, or just dungarees, T-shirts or trousers. The high-quality trousers, in addition to protecting, are particularly comfortable due to the many pockets present, suitable for keeping any type of tool with you, because they are adequately roomy and reinforced.

Work gloves for DIY

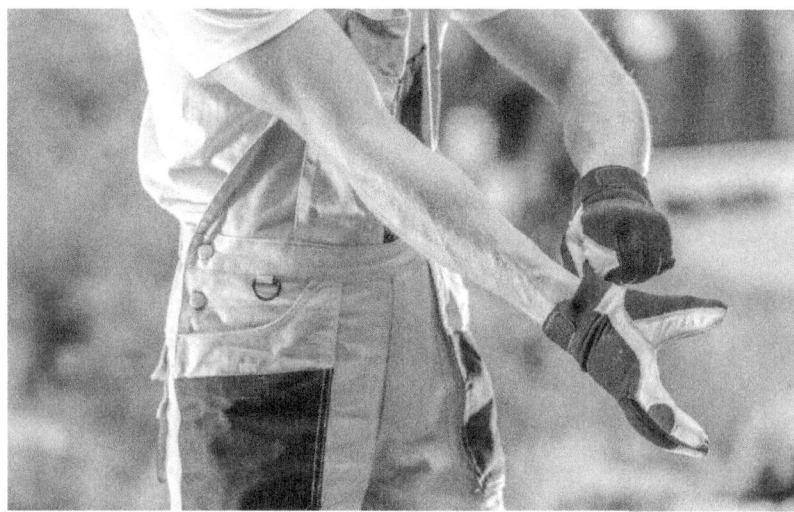

They are indispensable PPE for any renovation work, as they protect your hands from abrasions, tears, contact with chemicals, oils, greases and so on.

Generally, these PPE are made of cotton and leather and are equipped with latex, PVC, nitrile and butyl inserts: choosing the right gloves depends on the type of renovation work you are going to carry out.

Among the work gloves that you can find on the market, both disposable and reusable, there are:

- ✓ Work gloves that protect you from contact - or radiation - from convective heat, fire and small splashes of molten metal.
- ✓ Work gloves that protect you from the cold due to climatic conditions or from contact with objects.
- ✓ Electrically insulating work gloves, which protect you from contact with live parts - also cover the forearms.
- ✓ Work gloves for healthcare environments that protect you from possible contamination; these types of gloves can be made from both vinyl and rubber.

So, for hand protection, the choice is really wide. Each model is suitable for any type of work. We start with simple latex gloves when working with glues, for example, which will not affect dexterity.

The situation is quite different if the DIY jobs will be gardening.

Thorn-proof gloves such as those in cowhide will be necessary for pruning.

Particularly suitable for pruning rose gardens, they are extremely safe and comfortable thanks to the adjustable forearm band.

If, on the other hand, you enjoy small wooden jobs with particularly sharp tools, it is a good idea to raise the bar even further with a pair of anti-cut work gloves that guarantee an excellent grip.

There are even gloves on the market, which have both high cut resistance but also an excellent grip and will even allow you to use the touch screen without having to take them off every time.

The safety shoes

Safety shoes are PPE designed to protect the feet.

Even if they are produced in different types, they are all equipped with:
- ✓ Steel toe cap for toe protection
- ✓ Heel that protects and absorbs shocks
- ✓ Anti-puncture plate that prevents cuts from sharp objects
- ✓ Oil resistant, non-slip and anti-static outsole to protect you from electric shock.

DIY jobs: hearing protection

Perhaps one of the last things you think about in home repair and improvement safety is protecting your hearing. It may seem strange, but a constant sound like that of a drill can cause considerable damage to the ear in the long run.

Staying hours and hours with these tools in operation can be really harmful. For this reason, the use of ear defenders is highly recommended.

Do it yourself home repairs: construction helmet

A construction helmet for do-it-yourself jobs might seem exaggerated but it's not. Even cleaning a gutter, for example, is a job that you can easily do yourself. Easy work, sure, but still done at potentially dangerous heights.

Helmets are essential PPE while carrying out renovation activities, as they protect you from damage caused by accidental impacts or falling materials from above.

For these motivations, this PPE is mandatory in some working environments. In addition, helmets protect you from the danger of crushing, offer you electrical and thermal insulation and defend you from splashes of molten metal due to welding, for example.

Helmets, in general, consist of a shell and an adjustable harness that serves to adapt them perfectly to the head.

Among the helmets available on the market, you can choose from the following types:

- ✓ Standard, consisting of an outer shell, a shock absorbing inner cap and a holding strap. These helmets protect you from bumps, falls, cuts and punctures.
- ✓ High-performance, in which the protective qualities of standard protective helmets are combined with adequate resistance to lateral pressures.
- ✓ With dielectric properties, i.e., resisting contact with electric current up to 1000 volts in alternating current and up to 1500 volts in direct current.
- ✓ Forestry, particularly useful for gardening jobs that require the use of tools such as chainsaws and brush cutters; in this case, the helmets are formed by protection for the head, for the face, for the eyes and by anti-noise work headphones.

Those just analyzed are the main PPE necessary for the restructuring. Depending on the type of refurbishment you need to carry out, you can also add extra protection for extra protection, such as knee pads and fall arrest harnesses, if you are working on a bridge renovating a facade or if you are on a rooftop.

Or the pruning of a pine tree, whose cones could accidentally come off and hit the worker. It is certainly not the writer's task to implement a policy of terror, but it is good to know that danger, even unexpected, is always around the corner even in the simplest of DIY jobs in the garden.

When purchasing a safety helmet, the key thing to check is that it is approved to US government safety standards.

Dust masks for DIY

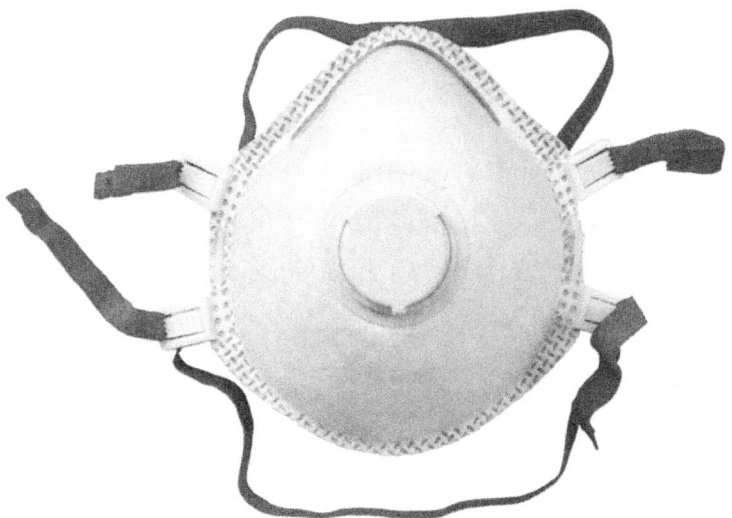

We've been hearing about masks for months now, but dust masks are a whole other story. In fact, these are particularly useful for all the do-it-yourself jobs that will produce volatile substances.

This personal protective equipment is of different types. They also exist with a built-in valve or activated carbon filters depending on the degree of protection they must guarantee against more or less toxic dusts and mists.

The quality of the product must be such as to offer a lifetime guarantee.

If this protection seems exaggerated, however, it will be enough to think of a rather common job, such as painting the walls of the house.

Removing the old paint will create a lot of extremely harmful volatile dust. The same applies when painting a surface using a spray gun.

Safety goggles

Finally, all that remains is to preserve your eyes from any particles or splinters.

Work glasses are PPE for eye and face protection from splinters, debris, gases, liquids, drops and dust, while you cut, weld and carry out all the paperwork required by the renovation you are dealing with.

Among the types of work glasses, you can choose between:
- ✓ Work glasses with or without screens placed on the sides.
- ✓ Goggles in the shape of a mask.
- ✓ Visor work glasses.
- ✓ Face shields that also protect the forehead and head.
- ✓ Hand shields, mostly used for welding.

The use of safety glasses or a protective mask must guarantee maximum comfort, without altering your vision.

Especially useful in work with wood, paint and iron, glasses while doing DIY jobs must also be very comfortable, anti-fog and be perfectly safe.

Here too, choose those of excellent quality because they offer excellent protection from dust, scratches and possible splashes, but above all they are very comfortable to use even if worn over ordinary eyeglasses.

Hand wash

A good hand washing paste must always be available as the skin can meet variously harmful substances, but also just with dirt, grease, sludge.

Fire extinguisher

Even if in a very limited form, in a home laboratory there is the risk of triggering a fire, for example when arc welding is carried out and the incandescent slag is projected into the surrounding space. personal protective equipment Among the personal protective equipment it is worth keeping a fire extinguisher, possibly near the entrance door and preferably of the CO_2 type, the jet of which extinguishes the fire by subtracting oxygen from combustion, without causing damage. Learning how to use the fire extinguisher is essential in order not to be caught unprepared in case of need. To make it functional, to remove the security seal is required. Where the wind is blowing, it is important to direct the jet of the fire extinguisher in the same direction as the wind.

Basic safety procedures

Basically, we are already telling you in the previous paragraph that it is essential to work in perfect safety! It is absolutely not a factor to be overlooked, renovating a do-it-yourself home does not mean being able to carry out the activities without a helmet or wearing comfortable slippers, but the opposite. In fact, precisely because you are not fully expert in the work, you must have your own safety and health at heart. For this, in addition to the right equipment, it is necessary to know some basic safety procedures.

Here are some basic guidelines for home repair safety:

- ✓ Renovation works therefore require extreme attention, everything needs its waiting times, whether they are short or long, but the most important thing to respect is safety. In the first place, the construction site must be totally arranged and tidy, nothing must be left to chance, documents, tools, materials, cleanliness, order and determination, avoiding sudden changes of ideas.
- ✓ If you have to carry out renovation work, you cannot do without the PPE (Personal Protective Equipment) we have just mentioned above, in order not to risk serious injuries.
- ✓ Whether you are a novice or an experienced worker, these devices will keep you safe from any accidents which, despite the attention you can pay to your safety, can happen accidentally while you are indulging in your work or your favorite hobbies. Being at home and working on the DIY home renovation does not mean neglecting safety, so no work done in shorts or flip flops, having the correct clothing is important, so don't forget a helmet and overalls.
- ✓ The injuries you could face if you don't use PPE are many, as you can risk:
  - o Cut yourself using tools such as a chainsaw, shears or other blunt objects.
  - o Irritate the respiratory tract or eyes due to contact with chemical or corrosive substances.
  - o Burning yourself with tools such as a welding machine or blowtorch.
  - o Falling from scaffolding or a roof, risking serious injury.
  - o Crush your fingers with a hammer.

- o   Lacerate a foot accidentally stepped on a nail.

    For this reason, given the high number of cases in which underestimating the use of PPE leads to serious consequences, we strongly recommend their use.
- ✓ To these PPE must be added the anti-fall protections, such as harnesses, which are used to save you from any falls when you work at a height that can cause more or less serious trauma in the event of a fall, whether it is a staircase, a terrace or the roof of your home if you are fitting a canopy cover, for example.
- ✓ Anyone who renovates a house on his own must have adequate technical skills and knowledge and be able to recognize materials that contain dangerous substances, such as asbestos. For do-it-yourself you need well-ventilated rooms.
- ✓ Living spaces are not suitable for activities that generate a lot of pollutant emissions, such as manual work and DIY. It would be ideal to have well-ventilated workshops or cellars equipped for this purpose in case paints, thinners or glues that release volatile organic compounds have to be used. These rooms are also suitable for sawing, filing and polishing activities which can rapidly produce unhealthy dust.
- ✓ If you want to renovate your own home, you should first acquire the necessary building knowledge and prefer products that generate low emissions. Eco and organic labels can help you choose. It should not be forgotten that environmentally friendly products must also be combined and treated correctly. Furthermore, all the products that need to dry need times of exposure to the air which vary from several days to several weeks.
- ✓ During renovation work, products that are dangerous to health and the environment are often encountered. In houses built or renovated in the previous decades, for example, materials containing asbestos can be found. Other problematic substances in buildings include PCBs in joint sealants, lead in old paints and varnishes, tar oil in parquet glue and insulating foils.
- ✓ If during a check carried out by the competent bodies something should be illegal, not compliant with the law, missing or inadequate such as safety, the project and the documentation, the risk is that of incurring heavy penalties with the opening of legal proceedings.

Electrical safety

In general, when it comes to the safety of home repairs in relation to electrical systems we have that:

For the installation, transformation and expansion of electrical systems, a project must always be drawn up:
- ✓ Electricity is essential for living in a home. It is not only used for lighting but to employ various appliances and devices. The system must be designed down to the smallest detail with

particular attention to safety. A state-of-the-art electrical system allows you to enjoy a comfortable and well-equipped home.

- ✓ This project is drafted by a registered professional (architects, engineers, surveyors, experts
- ✓ Projects must comply with current regulations.
- ✓ At the end of the execution of the system, the declaration of conformity must be issued containing at least the relationship with the type of materials used and the project.
- ✓ This declaration must also be issued in the case of partial execution of plants, relating only to the part built.
- ✓ A series of interventions are required to create a new electrical system but also to modify an already installed one. The first thing you need to do is map out the tracks, marking the points to be excavated on the wall. The groove for the passage of the cables is then made and then the boxes and fruit-holder boxes are positioned.
- ✓ We continue with the positioning of the tubes that protect the cables and the electric wires are passed through. At the end the traces are closed, and the walls are restored. Finally, we proceed with the connection of the devices and the wiring of the junction boxes.
- ✓ The customer is obliged to entrust the execution of the systems only to these companies.

To understand: in an electrical system, redoing the system does not mean pulling out the old cables, putting new ones in the same conduits and replacing inserts and plates (this is a sort of bringing it up to standard... even if it wouldn't really be up to standard). Redoing an electrical system means completely dismantling the old system, breaking the walls to let the new conduits pass, putting in new cables, outlets, switches, redoing the electrical panel.

Anyway, home repair electrical safety is of paramount importance when working with electrical systems. Here are some tips to help you stay safe:

- ✓ Turn off the power: Before you start any electrical repair work, make sure that the power to the area you are working on is turned off. You can do it by switching off the circuit breaker or taking away the fuse from the circuit.
- ✓ Use proper tools: Employ only tools and equipment that are adapt for electrical work. Be quite sure they are in good condition, and that you know how to use them properly.
- ✓ Check for damage: Inspect all wires, cables, and cords for damage before starting any repair work. If you find any damage, replace the damaged parts immediately.
- ✓ Avoid water: Keep all electrical tools and equipment away from water. Do not touch electrical equipment with wet hands (never), and make sure the area you are working in is dry.
- ✓ Don't overload circuits: Do not overload circuits by plugging in too many appliances or devices. This can bring to overheating and result in electrical fires.

By following these tips, you can ensure that you stay safe while making repairs to your home's electrical system.

Ladder safety

Ladders are an essential tool for home repairs, but they can also pose a safety risk if not used properly. Here are some ladder safety tips to keep in mind:

- ✓ **Choose the right ladder for the job:** Make sure the ladder you use is appropriate for the task at hand. For example, if you need to reach a high area, choose a ladder that is tall enough to reach it without standing on the top rungs.
- ✓ **Inspect the ladder before use**: Verify the ladder for any damage or defects, like cracks, loose screws or hinges, and worn-out rungs. Never utilize a damaged ladder.
- ✓ **Set up the ladder on a level surface:** be always sure the ground is level and stable before placing the ladder. Use a ladder stabilizer or leg levelers if necessary.
- ✓ **Make the ladder secure:** employ a ladder stabilizer or tie the ladder to a fixed object to avoid any tipping over.
- ✓ **Maintain three points of contact**: When climbing the ladder, always maintain three points of contact, either two hands and one foot or two feet and one hand.
- ✓ **Use a tool belt or bucket**: your hands should free by employing a tool belt or bucket to hold your tools.
- ✓ **Follow weight capacity guidelines**: Ladders have weight capacity guidelines that should be followed. Do not exceed the weight limit of the ladder.
- ✓ **Don't use the top rungs:** Never stand on the top rungs or the paint shelf of a ladder. They are not designed to support your weight.
- ✓ **Don't work in hazardous weather conditions**: Avoid using ladders in hazardous weather conditions, such as strong winds, rain, or snow.

Working with power tools

Working with power tools during home repairs can be dangerous if not done properly. Here are some tips to help you stay safe while using power tools:

- ✓ **Read the manual**: Always read the manual that comes with the power tool before using it. This will be useful for understanding how to use it safely and effectively.
- ✓ **Wear protective gear:** don't forget hearing protection, safety glasses and properly gloves to prevent injuries from flying debris, dust, or noise.
- ✓ **Inspect the tool**: Before using the power tool, check it for damage or wear and tear, such as frayed cords, cracked or bent parts, or loose screws or bolts. Never use a damaged tool.
- ✓ **Use the right tool for the job:** Use the right tool for the job and make sure it is appropriate for the material you are working with.
- ✓ **Secure the workpiece:** Secure the workpiece to prevent it from moving while you work. This can prevent accidents and injuries.
- ✓ **Keep your workspace clean and organized:** Keep your workspace clean and organized to prevent accidents and injuries. Try to don't' place cords and cables are not in the way, but also be sure to have the right space to work in safety way.
- ✓ **Turn off the tool when not in use:** Always turn off the power tool when you are not using it. This will prevent accidental starts and help extend the life of the tool.

Working with hazardous materials

Finally, as regards the safety of materials when you decide to do home repair work, know that dangerous materials in construction, the dangerous substances and products that are mostly used in construction are: adhesives (adhesives for floors, walls and ceilings); additives for concrete and cement mortars: accelerators, air entrainers, plasticizers, retarders; masonry cleaners: anti-algae, anti-mold, paint strippers, cleaners for greasy products (tar, asphalt, etc.); protective and decorative treatments of masonry: waterproofing products and membranes, anti-mold products; protective and decorative treatments of metals such as anti-rust paints and base coats; protective and decorative treatments of wood: top coats and base coats, paint strippers and paints for interiors and exteriors; finishing treatments for floors: waterproofing membranes, finishing varnishes, hardeners, levelers, fillers and anti-dust treatments; formwork treatments: formwork paints, release agents, surface retarders; resin-based, silicate-based and foam-based plasters; solvents. Before being used, these products must be analyzed and provided with certificates issued by accredited laboratories. By accreditation of a test laboratory, we mean the formal recognition of the technical competence of the laboratory in carrying out certain tests issued by a third party. Also, in this case it is good, therefore, whenever you have to intervene, in any type of work, to prevent risks with some simple precautions and using the right personal protective equipment.

Do-it-yourself personal protective equipment allows you to carry out DIY work in complete safety by protecting the most exposed parts of the body Do-it-yourself jobs involving home maintenance, whether repairs, decoration or various bricolage, are not entirely risk-free activities, as they involve the use of manual and motorized tools, more or less harmful substances, more or less dangerous. It is good, therefore, whenever you have to intervene, in any type of work, to prevent risks with some simple precautions and using the right personal protective equipment. In any case, it is always an excellent solution to carefully read the instructions for use before using any type of chemical product.

It is also useful to know that the rooms in which you work must be ventilated as much as possible, especially when painting, sanding or using solvents.

With all there is to know about security, our first chapter closes. We will see, in the second part of this guide, which are the most useful and necessary tools and materials to start your repair and improvement work on your home.

PART 2: Tools and Materials

This chapter covers the essential tools that readers will need to have in their toolkit in order to tackle various home repair and improvement projects. It includes an overview of different types of tools, such as hand tools, power tools, and specialty tools, and explains when and how to use them. The chapter also covers the importance of proper tool maintenance and storage to ensure that tools remain in good working condition.

It covers the different types of materials that readers will need to have on hand for various home repair and improvement projects, such as lumber, drywall, insulation, and electrical wiring. The chapter also covers how to select the right materials for specific projects and how to properly store and handle them. Additionally, the chapter covers sustainability considerations for selecting environmentally friendly materials, as well as cost-effective options for readers who are working with a budget. By understanding the different materials available and how to use them, readers will be better equipped to tackle a variety of home repair and improvement projects.

Essential tools for home repairs and improvement

Increasingly, in case of need, people choose low-cost solutions such as do-it-yourself to carry out small repair and improvement jobs at home. It is possible to devote oneself to ordinary maintenance quickly and well having a set of tools, to deal with different situations. The passion for DIY jobs will do the rest but beware of haste and confusion that can complicate things. What should never be missing at home for manual work? What can't be missing:

- ✓ Drill (better with disengageable percussion and with speed adjustment, possibly with reversible rotation); plus, related masonry, iron and wood drill bits
- ✓ Phillips and flat tip screwdrivers
- ✓ Collet (universal)
- ✓ Parrot key
- ✓ Nippers (side cutter)
- ✓ Two hammers, one small and one large
- ✓ Set with small pliers and mini precision screwdrivers
- ✓ Some fixed wrench (from n 8 to 13)
- ✓ Allen key set
- ✓ Assortment of screws and nails
- ✓ Wall plugs of various sizes
- ✓ Small hacksaw with blades for iron
- ✓ Portable workshop lamp
- ✓ 5m rollable measuring tape and rigid measuring tape

We will try to analyze some of these tools.

The toolbox

To always have everything at hand and keep your DIY tools tidy, the best thing is to store them in the toolbox. It can be composed of metal or plastic; it is resistant and full of compartments. You buy it already complete, or you buy it empty, to be customized over time according to the various fields (plumbing, gardening, carpentry). The first suggestion for successfully dealing with small "emergency" operations is to choose the tools without having savings as the sole objective. There are many proposals for DIY tools on the market, from the simplest low-cost models to the super-performing ones for professionals. Even the less experienced technicians advise to always focus on a few indispensable but good quality pieces. This is not only to prevent tools from being damaged at the slightest effort, but also because it is easier to carry out the work with the right tools. If as far as the original equipment is concerned, you can limit yourself to a few tools, it is instead important to establish a precise place where to place them, whether you have a simple box to store in a wardrobe door, or whether you can count on a dedicated room, such as a storage room or a cellar, so as to always have them ready and close at hand.

For the cassette, many models

There are those who prefer to buy it empty and personally choose the tools and those who, on the other hand, opt for already complete solutions, so as to be able to have a basic equipment that can eventually be integrated over time, according to specific needs. The offer is vast, even in terms of prices. Toolboxes are made of metal or plastic: with the same dimensions and organization of the internal compartments, between those in metal and those in plastic what makes the difference is the weight and resistance. Then there are the canvas bags, a simplified version with minimal equipment.

To complete the kit, it is advisable to acquire commonly used spare parts, such as: gaskets for taps, spare light bulbs, plumber's clamps, electrical plugs. By purchasing doubles, if the problem occurs again, you are already supplied and can intervene promptly.

Cutter

Choose a cutter, with sharp and retractable blades: you need a sturdy one, better to avoid those for stationery work.

Hacksaw or metal scissors

Made of steel, with a rigid plastic handle, they are useful for cutting thick wire and metal pipes.

Double meter

Made of wood, divided into 10 foldable rods, it is comfortable because once opened and stretched out it does not flex.

Torch

There are LED models that work with traditional batteries or with rechargeable batteries.

Electrician's scissors

It is used to cut and uncover electric wires: choose it with insulated handles, for greater safety.

Adhesive product

Glue or double-sided tape, suitable for gluing or fixing different materials. The price may change according to the kind of product.

Lubricant

A spray liquid is ideal for lubricating metal surfaces, to eliminate friction and facilitate the release of screws or bolts.

Bubble level

It is a measuring tool employed to establish the slope of a surface with respect to a horizontal reference plane. It is useful, for example, in case you need to fix a shelf on the wall. There are also levels with three bubbles: 1 horizontal, 1 vertical, 1 inclined at 45°. They often have a centimeter on one side to help with measurements.

Screwdriver set

You will need a set of screwdrivers.

In any case, among all hand tools, screwdrivers are the ones that are experiencing the most important evolution. Thinking of a screwdriver as a handle connected to a rod that ends with a tip is extremely simplistic. Let's start with the tip: have you noticed that the straight slotted screws are slowly disappearing? All due to the advent of electric screwdrivers whose tip, driven rapidly by the motor, escapes from the head of the screw if it has a straight slot, while it remains firmly there if it has a cross slot. The same goes for hand screwdrivers.

Screwdriver handles

The handles have become in soft material that gently accompany the hand. The stems are made of high-quality steel and the tips (flat or cross) are made of extra hard material. Naturally we are talking about quality screwdrivers and not the stall ones which, we remind you, are dangerous and last for the space of a few screwing. At home we must have a small supply of at least three screwdrivers with a flat tip and three with a cross tip of different sizes.

Choose at least 3-4 of each type, with ergonomic and non-slip handles. Better if they have a long blade, to reach less accessible points (the small ones will be used for precision work).

In any case, you should know that:

- ✓ The handle is a fundamental element of the screwdriver as it affects the practicality of use of the tool. Visible in the photo are T-handle, traditional cylindrical, square for improved grip and ergonomic soft.

- ✓ Screwdrivers for electric or electronic use have an insulated handle that is very elongated compared to the metal stem, to reduce the risk of contact.
- ✓ The traditional wooden handle gives way to plastic materials shaped according to the shape of the hand or knurled to improve grip. The high-quality screwdrivers are equipped with "soft" handles that are particularly respectful of the hands and fingers.
- ✓ A hexagonal crown placed at the base of the stem serves as a socket for a fork wrench and allows a great torsion force to be exerted on the tool, useful for starting a difficult unscrewing.

Screwdrivers – Phillips or Pozidrive?

We call them Phillips screwdrivers, but technically they fall into two families: Phillips and Pozidrive. The former has slightly conical tip wings. The latter have flat wings and have a notch that facilitates their centering on the head of the screw. The two types should be used on screws with relative notches, but they can be interchangeable even if screwing (or unscrewing) is a little less easy. However, both do not escape from the screw head during action.

Screwdriver bits

To have bits of different sizes available without having to equip themselves with the relative screwdriver, the "bits" (or "inserts") were invented: short bits with a hexagonal connection that can be inserted into the chucks of screwdrivers and into the appropriate universal screwdrivers equipped with a stem with insert holder recess. Typically, the bits are magnetized to facilitate contact with the screw. Replacing the screwdriver in the bit holder is very simple, just screw the chuck. The short bits are used with the manual bit holder or with ratchet wrenches, the double-ended ones only with chuck screwdrivers.

Screwdriver set

All the manufacturers also offer the bits in series which include bits of different kinds and a magnetic extension that allows you to use the short bits with screwdrivers. The assortments of bits are very convenient as initial equipment. Also very practical is the screwdriver with bit holder which has a small bit magazine in the handle that allows you to quickly switch from one type of screw to another.

Some pliers, the most versatile tool

Among the do-it-yourself tools, undoubtedly the most versatile is the pliers, which in fact is present in practically all homes. It can be used for interventions in the mechanical field or for carpentry work. The adjustable 'parrot' type, which tightens or tightens, is mainly used for hydraulic maintenance.

English keys

It will also be useful to always have a set of wrenches (indicatively from 8 to 13) close at hand in the toolbox, since these are do-it-yourself tools that can be adapted to many different needs.

Rollable measuring tape

Taking the measurements well only apparently seems like a simple and banal gesture: it is essential to avoid unpleasant surprises. Equip yourself with a 5–10-meter roll-up tape measure, in order to check and double-check that everything is in its place.

Drill

To dedicate yourself to the care of walls and masonry, choose a percussion drill equipped with a screwdriver function: it will allow you to screw in/unscrew any screw very quickly. It must have tips suitable for any job and surface (wall, iron, wood).

The ladder

To reach different heights, interpreting the specific need for intervention each time, the essential thing is to buy an extendable ladder. It can be used for DIY but also for any domestic operation 'in height'.

Level

If you intend to install suspended shelves or showcases in the living room or bedroom, it will be important to check the relative slopes with a spirit level. Better to choose a graduated model, to obtain greater precision.

How it's done

The one normally used in construction is made up of a rectangular section aluminum tubular, with a perfectly smooth face, of variable length, usually between 20 and 150 cm, which encloses one or more cylindrical vials containing a liquid, in which a bubble is left of air. In the simpler models, suitable for the do-it-yourself field, the only vial is arranged in the direction of the length, the more complete and professional ones also incorporate a perpendicular vial to this and one at 45° to check the inclinations. They can be equipped with a magnet, to remain supported by themselves on metal surfaces, and with a millimeter scale for measurements.

What is it for

It is used to verify flatness, perpendicularity, for the mutual alignment of elements (pictures, tiles, wall units), but also to give the right slope to some elements, such as the horizontal sections of the drainpipes, the external floors, the drainage channels.

How to use

By placing the level with the only smooth side on a surface, the air bubble, according to a physical principle, is positioned at the zenith point, i.e., the one furthest from the earth's plane. The surface is exactly horizontal (or vertical) when the bubble is located within the central area of the vial delimited by two notches, otherwise it is necessary to make the necessary corrections to achieve this condition. The survey is valid only in the length direction, therefore, having to verify the flatness of an entire surface, the spirit level must also be placed in a perpendicular position to the previous one, to obtain precision in both directions. This is typical of the case of cement screeds, or when you have to place an upright or erect a wall whose verticality must be checked on two faces that form a 90° angle.

Clothing

We have already pointed this out several times in the previous chapter. Moving safely is essential when dealing with maintenance work. You will need protective gloves and goggles but also safety shoes depending on the particular situation. Choose clothing with lots of pockets for storing utensils.

Hammer

It consists of a more or less long handle, made of wood, plastic or steel with a covered grip, and a head that has a different shape depending on the use. In the mallets it is stocky and symmetrical, while in the more common hammers there is a "mouth", the flat striking part, and a "pen", placed on the other. The latter can be linear or curved, compact or forked as in carpenter's hammers, with a nail-removing function. In a DIY workshop it is good to have hammers of different shapes and weights.

What is it for

Among the various types of hammers, those for carpenters, together with those for carpenters, are the classic hammers used for planting and for removing nails. Then there are demolition hammers (mallets), hammers with a rubber, wood or plastic head used for chiseling or to avoid damaging surfaces, with a ball-shaped mouth for pounding sheet metal and bodywork, hammers with a thinner mouth and head for tilers, for bricklayers, for welders, for upholsterers and for framers.

How to use

The hammer is held in the lower part of the handle, the dimensions of which are related to the weight of the head to ensure optimal balance. The movement of the arm must ensure that the flat part of the mouth is perpendicular to the nail to be planted, so that it penetrates vertically, without bending. The hammer must be chosen well as the weight and shape of the mouth must be related to the size and nature of both the nail and the material in which it is to be driven.

Lamp with hook

To work peacefully even in outdoor situations or in poor lighting, it will be useful to have a lamp that can be transported with a hook. Once hung your hands will be free.

Types of fasteners and hardware

In uncertain economic times like this one we're living through; you may need to save up for minor home repairs. Resorting to DIY in these cases could in fact succeed in the dual purpose of saving you time and money!

However, in order to carry out these small repairs, it is necessary to have the right fastening tools and DIY hardware.

If you have decided to jump into the world of hardware and fastener for the repair and embellishment of your home, there are thousands of items available: from products for the floor to those for the fireplace, from tools for the garden to power tools, from solutions for painting a wall to the tools for safety. The objects and furniture that can be repaired or built do not count.

Hardware types

However, experience teaches us that some work tools are more useful than others, as they are designed to address multiple needs. We have identified 4 absolutely unmissable work & do-it-yourself tools: for those who want to start off on the right foot, this list can only be a valuable handbook.

1. **A Dremel 4000 Platinum Edition**: The Dremel 4000 is a multi-tool with great performance. Inside the case there is space for the Dremel 4000 with EZ Twist cap, 6 accessories and 128 original accessories for high precision work. In addition, an information DVD and an instruction manual provide valuable advice on operating the device. Professionals, artisans and do-it-yourself enthusiasts will find the Dremel 4000 a valid ally in every situation. Limited Platinum Edition.
2. **A Fein Multimaster Start:** on our corporate website we have dedicated an entire page to the Fein Multimaster with 2 illustrative videos. This truly exceptional product represents the

perfect solution for interior renovation and refurbishment operations. A real investment to obtain impeccable results in the face of very simple management even for the less experienced.

3. **A Fretwork Moto Saw:** this is a small worktable with interchangeable saw for cutting a wide range of materials, from plywood to laminates, from plastic panels to Plexiglas, up to metals. The high ease of use ensures perfect alignment of the cut in both portable and stationary mode. The product comes complete with a sturdy and spacious case.
4. **Black & Decker drill/driver**: fourth but not least of the tools for work and do-it-yourself is the Black & Decker drill/driver. Equipped with lithium batteries and variable speed, this accessory has an ergonomic non-slip handle that ensures maximum control. Furthermore, the 24 adjustment points allow you to work on different materials and screw/drill on masonry, wood and metal.

Specific DIY tools or power tools

We advise you to use these tools only after acquiring some manual skills in DIY. In fact, these are tools such as:

- Sanders, milling machines, planes, hacksaws: which are more useful especially in working with wood.
- Welders, drills, staplers, riveters: these are do-it-yourself tools usually used for jobs that are carried out on furniture, shelves and shelves.

Fastener types

About types of fasteners that are commonly used in home repair projects, the common types are:

- **Screws:** Screws are threaded fasteners that are employed to hold objects together or to attach objects to surfaces. They come in many sizes and styles, including wood screws, machine screws, and sheet metal screws.
- **Nails:** Nails are pointed fasteners that are typically used to attach objects to wood. They come in many sizes and styles, including common nails, finishing nails, and brads.
- **Bolts:** are threaded fasteners that are employed with nuts to keep objects together. They can be found in many sizes and styles, such us carriage bolts, hex bolts, and lag bolts.
- **Anchors:** Anchors are fasteners that are used to attach objects to surfaces that cannot support the weight of the object on their own.
- **Rivets:** they are considered permanent fasteners that are employed to attach two pieces of metal together. They come in many styles, including solid rivets, blind rivets, and pop rivets.
- **Adhesive:** we are talking about substances that are utilized to join objects together.
- When choosing a fastener for a home repair project, it's essential to keep in mind the weight and size of the object being attached, as well as the type of surface it is being attached to.

Additionally, it's important to choose the right tool for the job, such as a screwdriver, hammer, or drill, to ensure that the fastener is properly installed.

Other tools
As other tools, for what concerning fastener we have:
- ✓ burglar-proof or spiral padlocks, locks for doors or gates, packaging materials such as protective cellophane coverings and bubble wrap sheets, lockable, fixed or flat-bed trolleys.
- ✓ From small metal fixings we have nails, bolts, screws, hinges, dowels up to larger DIY products.

Types of adhesives and sealants

Let's see now what types of adhesives and sealant are most helpful when it comes to deal with home repair and improvement. In fact, know that when you decide to carry out your repair work on your home, the use of suitable adhesives and sealants makes all the difference. These materials are precious allies to improve your home energy efficiency. They also help prevent the infiltration of water or humidity into the rooms. In this paragraph, we will give you the right advice and indications necessary to choose the best adhesive or sealant for specific uses in the building industry.

First of all, let's talk about sealant. What does it mean? What are the differences between sealant and adhesive? Let's try to answer these questions:

What is a sealant?
Polyurethane sealants are versatile sealants for construction. They can be employed on various surfaces such as wood, plastic, masonry, metal, aluminum, stucco and many others. They are waterproof and, making them the right choice for sealing the various cracks and joints found in outdoor structures.

Are polyurethane sealants and polyurethane adhesives the same?
While polyurethane sealants have some similar characteristics to their adhesive counterparts, they are not the same product and should not be used for the same applications and jobs. Polyurethane adhesives are made to give solidity to structures, while polyurethane sealants are designed to ensure both water and air resistant sealing and are also very flexible.

Sealants connect materials, sealing the joint between surfaces, and can also absorb movement within the joint itself. Sealants tend to create a weaker connection between two surfaces.

Adhesives have, as their main function, to join different building elements together. The sealant, on the other hand, has the main function of preventing the passage of liquids or gases between different environments.

There are certain types of work for which adhesive materials are better suited. For the others, the sealing ones. Example: When you are going to tile or join two pieces of drywall, you will use adhesive material. But when you have to thermally insulate a room or install sanitary fixtures in the bathroom, you will use sealing material.

Now that we have clarified the matter, let's see which type is right for you.

When deciding which type of adhesive or sealant to choose, you must keep in mind where to intervene and what kind of result to obtain. Materials, geometries and position of the elements to be joined can make the difference when choosing the type of material, you need. In fact, each junction point represents a critical point. The geometric or material irregularity between two building components can, in fact, lead to infiltrations or poor adhesion between the elements. To choose the most suitable adhesives and sealants, it is necessary to consider the shape of the joint and the materials of which the parts to be connected are made. Now let's see some types of adhesive or sealing materials.

The adhesives types

Here you are the most common kinds:

Stickers

Adhesive materials make rigid joints so that the glued pieces form a single piece. Among them, based on functions, materials and shapes, we can distinguish between contact adhesives, paste adhesives and polyurethane adhesives for wood.

Contact stickers:

This adhesive material is easy to use. In fact, you just need to spread it, with a brush or a spatula, on both surfaces you want to join. However, it is necessary to wait a few minutes before joining the parts to allow the solvents to evaporate and to facilitate the setting of the glue.

Paste stickers:

Mainly used for professional bonding, they are mainly used to join materials such as fiberglass, metal walls, tiles, textile walls, plasterboard, wood and plaster.

Polyurethane adhesives for wood:

These multifunctional materials resist humidity particularly well and are, for this reason, highly appreciated in the field of shipbuilding. This type of adhesive material is complementary to PVA glue.

Specific stickers:

They are materials that are used to glue certain materials or that are used for specific functions, such as ceramic tiles or carpet. This type of adhesive material is used successfully in soundproofing processes and thermal coatings.

The sealants types

The main feature of these materials is to prevent the passage of liquids, humidity and gases between the different building environments. However, they must also possess adhesive properties that allow them to perform this important function. These materials are essential to meet a building's need for energy efficiency. They can be based on silicones, acrylics or polyurethanes.

Silicone Sealant:

The main feature of this sealant is its transparency. Once applied, they cannot be painted. The materials on which they are usually applied have a porous composition. Many manufacturers add color pigments to encourage wider use of these materials. Ductile and easy to use, silicones are often used in the automotive sector.

Acrylic Sealant:

Particularly resistant to mold, they are highly appreciated for sealing tiles, bathtubs, swimming pools, bathroom fixtures and all those environments which are in constant contact with humidity, water and liquids. These materials become transparent when dried. Furthermore, this sealant in particular is highly appreciated in recovery work and in small domestic repairs. There are products based on acrylic sealant designed specifically for wood, and especially for parquet.

Polyurethane sealant or polyurethane foam:

This material polymerizes, i.e., hardens on contact with air. Of all the types of sealant, polyurethane foam is undoubtedly the most versatile. Mainly appreciated for insulating and bonding materials such as copper, galvanized sheet metal, aluminum fiberglass, stainless steel, painted sheet metal, plaster concrete, wood and air conditioning systems. Ductile, multiform and adaptable, polyurethane foam is widely used in shipbuilding.

Features to consider when choosing

It should be remembered that among the sticky materials it is necessary to distinguish between the sealant and the adhesive. The first creates elastic joints, whose main function is to insulate, protect and join different building parts. Its main function is, therefore, to prevent the passage of gases and liquids between one environment and another. The adhesive, for its part, serves to unite two different building elements in a stable form.

That said, when you're choosing an adhesive or sealant, you'll need to take a whole host of different factors into consideration. The setting time, which can be immediate or take a long time. Some are easy to dispense, while others need to be diluted with specific solvents. The materials, the shape, the position of the joints to be made are also fundamental factors when determining your choice. In addition to these, the cleanliness of the surface on which you will use your products: a poorly cleaned surface could alter and compromise the quality of the products which could therefore not work properly.

It is also good to remember that sealants are often used in combination with adhesive materials such as glues. In this way, the two main functions of the sealant and the adhesive are fully exploited. That is the seal between the elements and their perfect adhesion. Speaking of adhesive glues, it is important to consider two fundamental properties of these materials: the adhesion force and the cohesive force. By adhesion strength we mean the strength with which the glue is kept united to the material on which it is used. The expression cohesive force, on the other hand, refers to the ability of the glue to remain tied to itself.

There is no perfect adhesive or sealant, as each type is suitable for different materials, surfaces and uses.

Choosing the right paint and finishes

Let's complete this chapter with the right paint and finishes choice.

Painting allows you to give the interior and exterior of your home a whole new look in a relatively short amount of time. There are many different types of interior and exterior paint available. The type of surface you work on is also important: wood, metal, plaster, concrete, masonry or plastic. Every single material has its own specific features, and for this reason you will have to choose the right one or choose the right paint. You can opt for clear to opaque polish, or glossy and satin varnish. Many of these various types of paint are long lasting, subject to deterioration and natural wear and tear.

Paint is useful for exterior coatings that dry by evaporation or a solvent. They employ several types of materials, like additives, pigments, solvents and binding agents. These can be water-soluble (acrylic) or solvent-based (alkyd).

Always remember to use good quality brushes and rollers - they give a significantly better result.

In any case, choosing the best paint for walls is undoubtedly the first step to take when, for example, you intend to whitewash your home.

painting the house, yourself is certainly one of the most convenient methods to give a fresh and clean look to our home.

Painting the walls in itself is a fairly simple operation to carry out, it only requires a little time available (especially for the drying times between one coat and another), the right equipment and a little familiarity with colors and brushes.

Obviously, the result will depend a lot on your skill, but if you don't have to create walls with particular colors, with complex decorations or motifs, or use difficult painting techniques, but only whitewash, you can certainly venture out with the DIY.

Before starting, however, the best paint for walls should be chosen, i.e., the one that best meets your needs: is it better, therefore, a transpiring paint, a washable one or a thermal insulating one?

Let's see the different types and which one to choose to have cozy and design home interiors.

What type of paint to choose for improving your home?

On the market there are different types of paint for interior walls, among these there are:

1. Washable paint
2. The breathable paint
3. Thermal insulating paint

Washable paint, as the name suggests, is a type of paint that offers a series of advantages such as high opacity, ease of distribution on the walls and, above all, the possibility of being "washed" without damaging it because it is water repellent. It is suitable for any room in the house and, in particular, for those rooms where the walls get dirty, such as children's bedrooms, for example.

If you choose to whitewash your home using washable white paint, you can be sure you can clean it at any time.

Transpiring paint is the one that allows air to pass through, making the walls breathe and keeping humidity away: if you choose a transpiring white for the kitchen and bathroom, you will have a damp and mold-proof result (in many cases, however, it is advisable to first pass a specific anti-mold product to reinforce the result).

Finally, the thermal insulating paint is characterized by a particular mixture formed by microspheres which are placed between the wall and the paint, preventing the formation of condensation and keeping the walls safe from sudden changes in temperature.

In all three cases, obviously, whatever type of color you choose to paint the walls of your home, it is good to prepare the walls with sandpaper - to smooth them - closing any holes and cracks with putty. The end result, with smooth and uniform base walls, will be much better.

Now let's move on to the prices of interior paints. In reality, even for the same type of paint you can find very different prices: it all depends on the manufacturer's brand and therefore also on the quality of the paint.

Since it is the interior walls of the house, the advice is not to choose exclusively for a matter of savings, but to select not only the most suitable type of paint according to the space that needs to be painted, together with the quality of the paint itself.

Finishes choice

Finish and protective both belong to the macro category of protectives, in the sense that they are the last layer of our furniture, the one that will then remain in contact with the environment (internal or external depending).

Let's go into a little detail.

Today when we talk about Finishing referring to a product, we mean all those ready-made preparations that are found in DIY and paint factories.

They can be neutral or colored, usually depending on the essence of the wood (cherry, walnut, mahogany...), they are usually water-based and are rather milky, but when dried they become transparent.

General technical characteristics of the finishes

Let's see the main finishes features:
- ✓ They filter UV
- ✓ They don't turn yellow
- ✓ They are odorless
- ✓ They are water repellent (which does not mean waterproof!)
- ✓ They can be used both indoors and outdoors

Basically, in addition to enhancing the surface on which we are going to put them, they also have a protective function.

However, if we are faced with extreme or thorny situations, it is better to bring into play other products more specifically designed for a protective function which therefore turn out to be more resistant.

Here are some of the best-known protectors:
- ✓ Glazing
- ✓ Resins
- ✓ Flatting

The glaze is very resistant and has the characteristic of recreating a glass effect on the surface where it is applied.

The resins, depending on the brand and type, can be single or two-component, are generally water-based, have high resistance even outdoors. As a contraindication they are a little more expensive.

Flatting, mainly solvent-based, is excellent for outdoors because it has very high resistance (it is also used for doors and windows and boats to be clear), it is brilliant, and it really creates a film. At the end of the work the tools must be cleaned with solvents.

In most cases it is better to spread these products with a brush (with the exception of certain types of resins) so as to have greater control.

But let us remember that the protective, even if it were the best in the world, is not eternal and maintenance is very important.

As absolute advice we always tell you that it is much more convenient to remember cyclically to go over a protective product on the same product and to do maintenance rather than waiting for it to wear out and finding yourself with exposed wood, because at that point it will already be compromised.

This is particularly true for doors, shutters, tables and benches, summer chairs, in short, everything that is subject to atmospheric agents or situations of particular stress.

This second chapter has also come to an end. In the third part of this practical guide, we will deal with plumbing.

PART 3: Plumbing

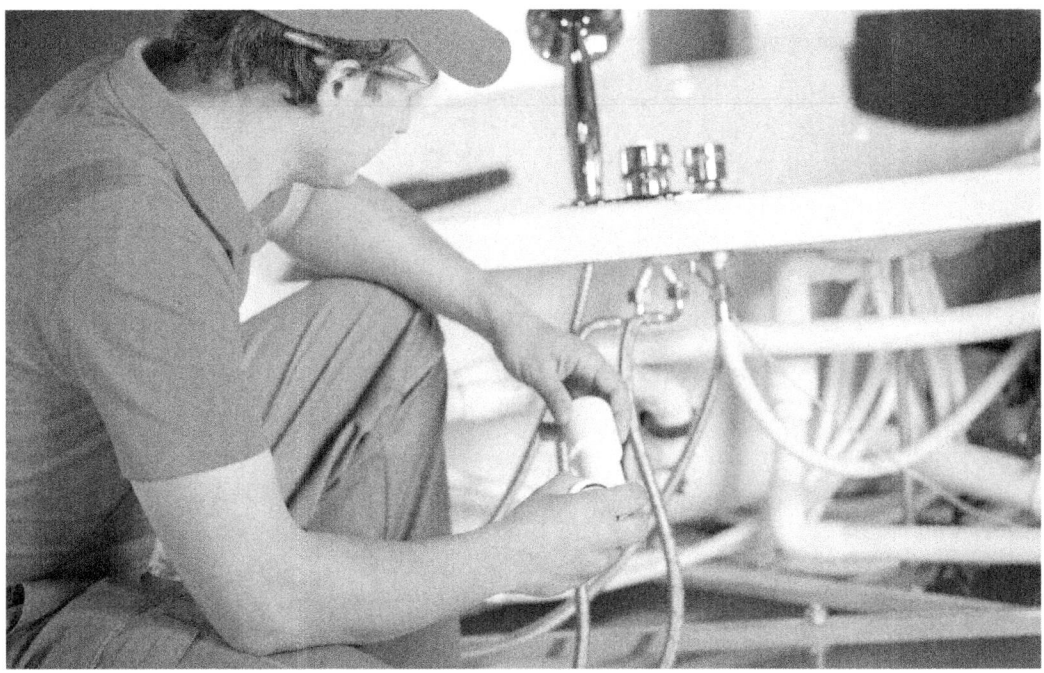

In this chapter, readers will learn how to fix common plumbing problems such as leaky faucets, clogged sinks, and running toilets. The chapter also covers more advanced plumbing tasks such as installing water filtration systems and garbage disposals.

Basic plumbing repairs

Let's start with the real basics of plumbing. The plumbing system is not only of fundamental importance for our everyday life, but its malfunction, or simple leaks can cause structural damage to buildings: we all know how much a single drop of water can gouge a rock.

But, talking about plumbing system, its functions are essentially two:

1. The distribution of food and sanitary water: drinking water.
2. The disposal of wastewater: black water, i.e., organic residues, soapy residues or even rain water.

Our plumbing systems consist of several parts:

- ✓ The adduction columns: through which the hydraulic system of the building is connected to the municipal aqueduct.
- ✓ The pipes: which carry the clear water to each individual room, and which convey the black water to the sewage system.
- ✓ Autoclave: it is not always present in all plumbing systems, but only when the water pressure is not enough to reach the upper floors of the buildings.
- ✓ The stopcock: of fundamental importance. The main tap has the function of isolating the water flows to and from the apartments.

- ✓ The manifold: it ensures the distribution of the condominium water between the various components of the domestic plumbing system.

The materials used and the types

Now let's see the materials with which a hydraulic system can be created, according to current regulations

- ✓ Galvanized steel
- ✓ Black steel
- ✓ Stainless steel
- ✓ Copper
- ✓ Polypropylene
- ✓ Multilayer material: composed of a polyethylene pipe covered with a layer of aluminum and another in plastic.

As far as equipment is concerned, we bet that your toolbox, thanks to the advice in the previous chapters, is well stocked, but before starting work, we advise you to make a small selection of everything you have and what you may have need.

Buying good quality tools guarantees us an easier and less unexpected job, so spend a little more money and choose wisely.

The plumber's essential tools, for being furthermore specific are:

- ✓ **Plunger:** The classic suction cup plunger
- ✓ **Reamer:** It is used to deburr the tube after cutting
- ✓ **Screwdrivers:** They can be cut or star
- ✓ **Gas trolley with cylinder:** it is the appliance used for all welding operations and when it is necessary to heat the surfaces to be worked.
- ✓ **Pipe clamp stand:** to tighten the pipes.
- ✓ **Wrench:** Allows you to adjust the wrench according to the size of the nut
- ✓ **Pipe wrench:** allows you to forcefully tighten the pipes to be rotated or the joints to be assembled and disassembled.
- ✓ **Fixed keys:** hydraulic pipes supply chain
- ✓ **Production chain:** it is used to thread pipes; during the threading work it is advisable to lubricate the pipe with cutting oil.
- ✓ **Plumbed Scissors:** robust and reliable
- ✓ Cutter for taps it is used to smooth the seat of the tap seals.
- ✓ **Swedish pipe wrench:** special pipe clamp
- ✓ **Limes:** for smoothing and cleaning metal surfaces after cutting; you need at least one flat and one round with a rat tail. Having them in various sizes is always useful.
- ✓ **Retractable metal meter:** bending spring

- ✓ **Spring for pipe benders:** it is introduced into the pipes before bending them with the pipe bending pliers so as to avoid crushing the pipe.
- ✓ **Plunger spring:** It slips into the clogged tube by rotating it by hand.
- ✓ **Pipe vice:** it is used to block the pipes during cutting, filing, boring, threading and welding operations.
- ✓ **Pipe expander pliers:** it is used to flare the copper pipes before making the joints with the quick couplings.
- ✓ **Packing nut pliers:** equipped with adjustable jaws, it is used to loosen or tighten small nuts located in difficult to access points.
- ✓ **Pipe bending pliers:** allows you to bend pipes with a diameter between 8 and 32 mm without great effort and without deforming the pipe itself
- ✓ **Vertical gripper:** to butt-tighten the pipes.
- ✓ **Gun for silicone cartridges:** it serves to evenly squeeze the silicone sealant out of the cartridge.
- ✓ **Steel punch:** to correctly assemble some hydraulic compression joints it is necessary to widen the mouth of the pipes to be connected.
- ✓ **Electric welding machine:** useful in the craftsman's arsenal and not just for plumbing work
- ✓ **Hole saw for holes:** it is an accessory to be mounted on the low-speed electric drill; it is used to drill large holes. Models with diameters of various sizes are on the market.
- ✓ **Metal hacksaw:** it is the useful tool for cutting pipes or other metal materials; there are different sizes, and it is good to have a small one and a large one with an adjustable bow.
- ✓ Wire brush and iron wool serves to clean metal surfaces.
- ✓ **Asbestos mat:** it is a piece of fabric with asbestos fibers to be placed behind the joints to be welded, to protect the surrounding areas from heat.
- ✓ **Pipe cutter:** it is the indispensable tool for perfectly cutting pipes at right angles.

Finding yourself without the right tool at the time of need is never pleasant!

Types of plumbing

There are two main types of plumbing that you can build:
1. Diverted hydraulic system: it consists of installing a main pipe that will be diverted for each individual user.
2. Manifold hydraulic system.

Diversion hydraulic system

Creating a diversion plumbing system is simple. As you can imagine, it is a question of installing a main pipe which will be diverted for each user via specific connectors called TEEs through which the water is brought to all domestic environments (bathroom, kitchen, terrace, laundry room, ...) and to all sanitary ware and appliances (washing machine and dishwasher).

The connection or junction points must not be visible but covered by tiles. This is the main disadvantage of this type of plumbing system, because in the event of a breakdown or leak it is necessary to break the floor or wall tiles.

Manifold hydraulic system

To create a hydraulic manifold system, it is necessary to install a hydraulic manifold in a special box on a wall to which all the utilities of the hydraulic system are then connected.

We have seen that creating a do-it-yourself water system is not child's play, but it is a job that requires not only good manual skills but also profound technical knowledge. In the next paragraphs we will expand the discussion even further.

Replacing faucets and fixtures

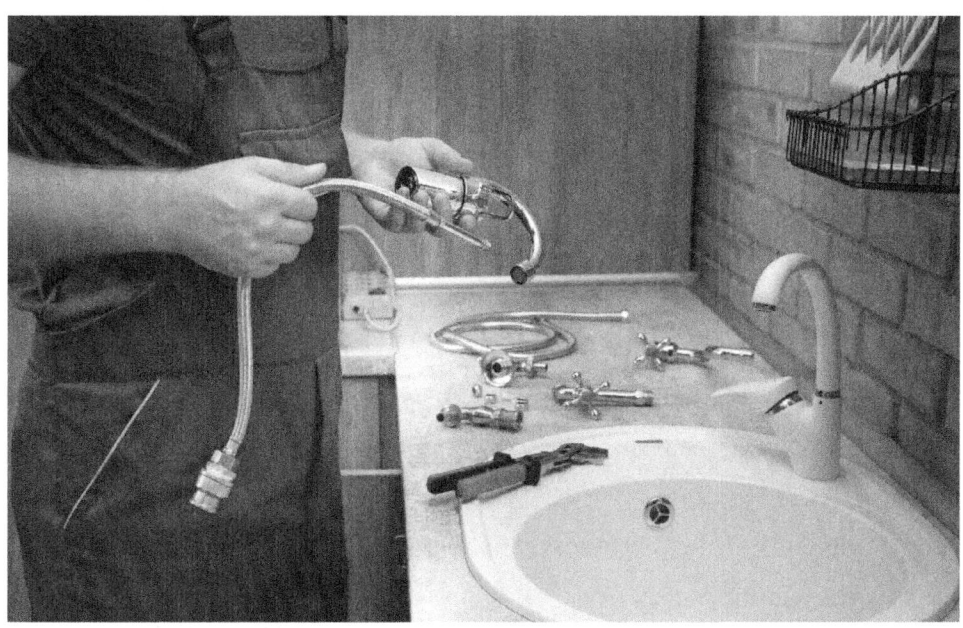

From the kitchen tap to the sink or bidet tap, it is not uncommon for taps and fixtures to be changed due to a leak or breakdown due to wear. For that below, we will offer you some useful tips.

How to change a do-it-yourself faucet?

Changing faucet becomes child's play if you know how to do it, a DIY guide for water leak proof repairs. We are in the middle of the night, and we hear a continuous drip that does not let us sleep. A situation that has happened to everyone and that can send you into panic if you don't know how to change the faucet. The solution is to have the right information and know all the things to do to solve this annoying and costly problem.

Changing the tap is also and above all an economic issue, consumption increases without us actually using the water we pay for. A leaky tap therefore becomes a priority if you care about the efficiency of your plumbing system, the maintenance of the taps you have carefully chosen for your home. Talking about just one type is wrong: the leaking faucet can be the one in the kitchen, the sink in the bathroom or the bidet or the shower.

Each of them must be treated in a specific way and this simple guide will provide you with all the indications and tips you need to do.

The first thing to do is take care of the faucet gasket replacement.

Faucet gasket replacement

The first cause of a leaking faucet is undoubtedly attributable to the deterioration of the gasket. A leaking tap is a waste: water is consumed unnecessarily, without underestimating the wear and tear of the tap which can cause definitive deterioration. The gasket, also called O-ring, is a small rubber circle that isolates the knob from the passage of water and also has the function of making operation softer and smoother.

Water, due to the substances it contains, deteriorates the components of the faucet but also the sanitary ware. The continuous drip stains and consumes the coating of the sanitary ware. The passage of water rich in calcium carbonate can further damage each component. Added to this are also the bad habits of overtightening the knobs. The action to be taken, before the irreparable happens, is to take care of replacing the tap gasket.

Turn off the water, you have to avoid unwanted water leaks. Get a rag, to prevent annoying accidents, and tools. A screwdriver and a wrench are tools required.

The gasket is located around the knobs and therefore you must disassemble them, removing the cap that covers them and proceed with the screwdriver to loosen the screw that holds it welded. Remove the knob and take care of the mobile body of the tap with a wrench of the right size. Unscrew the small nut holding the gasket in place and proceed to replace the gasket.

We have addressed one of the most frequent causes of the malfunction but there are other reasons that force you to fix the leaking faucet.

How to replace the sink faucet

As we have seen, changing the tap is a fairly simple operation. Repairing a leaking faucet is almost always a problem with the gaskets or the cartridge placed near the wall.

Make sure these elements are in perfect condition, only in this way will you be sure of solving the problem without having to call a plumber. Our information will also allow you to repair the bidet faucet.

How to replace the bidet faucet

If you have one, repairing the bidet faucet is an operation that requires the utmost attention because, unlike the rest of the faucets, it is equipped with an extra element: the aerator.

The aerator is a filter that fits inside the passage chamber and looks like a small net.

The limescale present in the water fills this filter with waste which clogs it and this leads to a leak. Changing the aerator is the only solution and, after turning off the water and plugging the drain, you can proceed with a parrot to loosen it and then proceed with your hands to replace it.

If, on the other hand, the filter is free and the leak corresponds to the gaskets, all you can do is disassemble, with the right size wrench, the tap with the knob whose screws are located underneath.

How to replace the shower faucet

Proceed only at this point with the replacement of the gaskets and once finished, take care of the reassembly. With these notions you can fix your shower faucet.

Repairing your shower faucet is easy if you own a model with knobs. In this case you can use the indications already present on changing the gaskets on the knobs.

If, on the other hand, you have a shower with a mixer at home, you can change the tap and carry out the necessary repairs to avoid the leak.

Turn off the water and get yourself an Allen key and a parrot. With these tools, first loosen the knob and remove it and then unscrew the cover.

Loosen the stud, with the help of a parrot, remove the ring nut that holds the cartridge, slide it out and proceed to clean it and the holes.

Replace the cartridge, if necessary, if not, you can keep the procedure with the reassembly.

How to replace the fixtures

Do you want to replace the fixtures in your home by relying on DIY? Find out how in this guide! We'll give you all the information you need to replace your fixtures, and you'll find out how to renovate the windows of your home with your own hands.

If you don't have some experience, and the right equipment, aluminum could be quite difficult to DIY.

In addition to the material necessary for the fixtures for your home, you will also need other ancillary materials for their construction, assembly and painting, including for example:
- ✓ Fixing dowels
- ✓ Sliding guides for the doors
- ✓ Hinges
- ✓ Window handles and locks
- ✓ Screw nails
- ✓ Paint

Replacing the fixtures in your home can be quite easy, especially if your doors and windows are standard sizes, and not too complicated to take apart and put back together. You will have to remove the doors, lifting them from their hinges, or from the tracks if they are of the sliding type, and then proceed with the removal of the frames of the fixtures, if you need to replace them too. The frames are generally solidly screwed to the counter-frames, which in turn are fixed to the masonry, and with the right equipment you will be able to disassemble and remove them, to install the new frames in their place. You will have to be quite precise in carrying out this operation, to avoid any slopes, and above all to perfectly insulate the internal environments from the outside. Once the frames have been installed, you can mount the doors of your new windows, checking again the perfect tightness of the closure, acting if necessary, on the adjustment screws, generally present in the windows.

Before attempting to replace the fixtures in your home, we advise you to evaluate whether your do-it-yourself knowledge is sufficient to carry out the job with your own means. The fixtures represent, for your home, the most important barrier from atmospheric agents, cold and external noise, and if you are not able to install them in a workmanlike manner, you risk obtaining a final result that is not entirely satisfactory, or worse still inadequate.

Fixing leaks and clogs

Now, let's see how to fix leaks and clogs:

How to fix leaky faucet

You've seen how above that adjust the faucet isn't such a difficult operation, if you have the right tips, you've also discovered one of the main reasons for replacing the faucet gasket.

Prolonged use and the wrong way to close the knobs lead to tearing of the gaskets but a leaking tap can have other causes and you need to know how to intervene.

The first thing to do is, without any doubt, to shut off the water so that it does not spread throughout the whole system. Then you need to get yourself a screwdriver, a special key for opening the handle.

Repairing a leaking faucet often means intervening on the mixer or on the handles and on the cartridge placed near the wall. A job that you can do yourself, with maximum safety without resorting to the help of a professional.

Turn off the water and proceed to discard the handle plug. Once raised you must unscrew the screw, you can use a screwdriver. If the operation is more difficult for you, you can purchase and use a special key.

You will you be able (only in this manner) to extract the cartridge and replace it but be careful to position it correctly, otherwise you could have new problems.

How to fix kitchen faucet

Now that you have all the right knowledge, you know how to repair a faucet, even the one in the kitchen.

Fixing your kitchen faucet isn't any more difficult than dealing with any other leak.
- ✓ The first thing to do is, as always, turn off the water and get the right tools.
- ✓ Remove the stud covering the handle and unscrew the locking screw and remove the knob.
- ✓ Only in this way will you be able to unscrew the tap body, the gasket tightening nut.
- ✓ Remove the worn gasket and insert the new gasket.
- ✓ Now that you know how to take care of the kitchen faucet, you can also fix the sink faucet.

How to fix clogs

To solve blockage and clogs problems in the plumbing line, there are several solutions available. Here are some common options for repairing blockages:
- ✓ **Use a plumber's snake:** A plumber's snake, also known as a "plumber's snake," is a long, flexible tool with a corkscrew-like auger on the end used to unclog drain lines. It is inserted into the clog and moved back and forth to break and remove the blockage.
- ✓ **Use a blockage remover:** A blockage remover is a chemical that can loosen blockage and clear the pipeline. These products are poured directly into the sink or bathtub and left to sit for a certain amount of time before rinsing off with hot water.
- ✓ **Use a suction cup:** A suction cup, also known as a plunger, is a rubber tool with a handle used to create negative pressure and remove obstruction from the pipeline.
- ✓ **Remove the siphon:** The siphon is the "U" shaped pipe under the sink or bathtub that avoids the sewer gases to flowing back into the home. Removing the siphon can help clear the blockage if it is in that area.
- ✓ It is important to note that when dealing with blockage problems, care must be taken with the chemicals used and proper handling of tools to avoid any damage to the pipes or health risks.

Installing a new toilet or sink

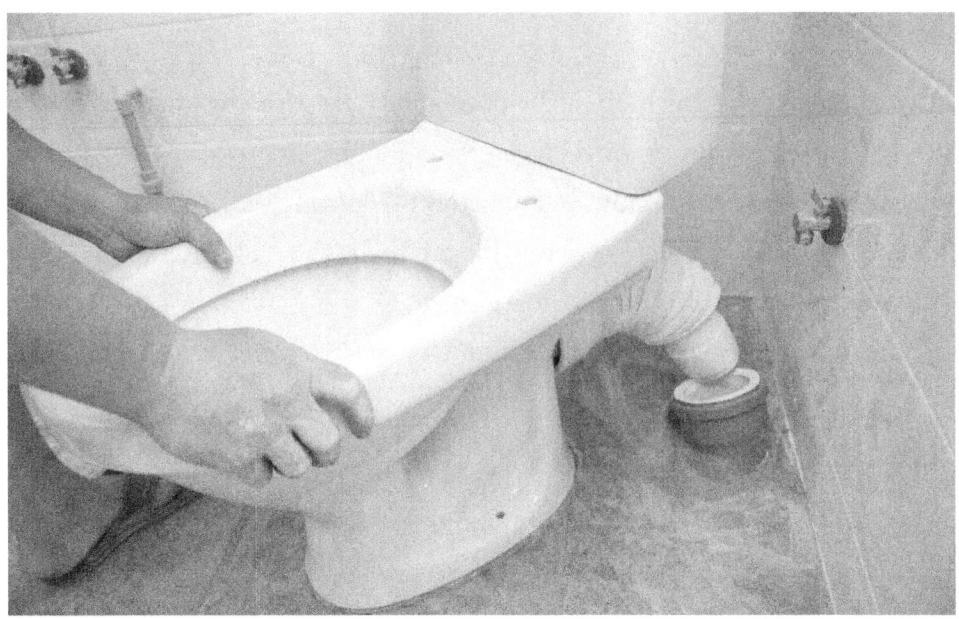

Now we will show you some useful trip for installing a new toilet or sink. Let's get it started!

Installing a new toilet

If you've bought a new toilet and want to do-it-yourself renovate the bathroom in your home, knowing how to install a toilet is a fundamental aspect, to avoid unpleasant accidents, or errors that can compromise the new purchased sanitary ware. And that's exactly what you will discover by reading this guide, in which you will find all the elements necessary to understand how to take care of the toilet installation yourself, step by step, in order to be able to carry out this operation in complete tranquility and safety.

Step 1 - Get rid of the old toilet to install a new toilet.

The first phase of the toilet installation procedure consists in taking care of the removal of the sanitary fixture to be replaced, taking all the necessary precautions to avoid accidents and to make sure that nothing is damaged.

Step 2 - Measure the distance of the toilet from the wall.

Before proceeding with the removal of your old toilet, it is necessary to know exactly the location of the toilet and the distance between the old toilet and the wall, but also with respect to the current and eventual position of your future furniture, to understand which it will have to be precisely the position, direction and more generally the location of your new toilet.

Step 3 - Turn off the water completely.

It may seem obvious to you, but it is better to specify it: before proceeding with any operational phase, the first thing to do is to close the terrestrial water key, to prevent this bathroom furniture object from continuing to collect water material that you will have to remove in any case completely before removing the toilet from the pipes.

Step 4 - Flush the drain and remove any remaining water from the old toilet.

After closing the land key, to remove any residual water from the toilet that you are about to remove, flush the toilet to completely empty the water pan as well. Be very careful to repeat this procedure as many times as necessary, until the total removal of liquids is obtained, to avoid unpleasant and unexpected water leaks which can significantly lengthen the time needed to complete the job.

Step 5 - For toilet assembly it is essential to use the protections.

This recommendation must be followed from this phase of the work onwards, because, as you probably already know, the toilet is an object particularly rich in bacteria and, if you do not manage each phase of this process correctly, or simply something unexpected should arise, you can, using the appropriate protections, avoid inhaling, touching or coming into direct contact with fumes, bacteria and bad smells.

Step 6 - Loosen the bolts holding the old toilet.

After wearing the necessary protections to install a toilet starting from the removal of its predecessor, it is important to carefully loosen each bolt and removable fixing element of the toilet bowl that you are about to replace, starting, if your toilet has this conformation, from the water tank, to avoid making the founding base of this object too unstable, risking falling parts of the toilet which can cause damage to the floor.

Step 7 - Disconnect the pipes that connect the toilet to the water.

At this stage, you will have to take care and concern yourself with disconnecting any connecting water pipes and connecting the toilet and water tank to any pipes. It is essential to carry out this step with particular caution, because, except in rare cases where it should be necessary, the water cables are not replaced and therefore they will be the same ones you are going to install in your new toilet.

Step 8 - Remove the water tank from the toilet (only if you have a toilet of this type)

This is a step designed for all toilets equipped with an integrated cistern. Since toilets without cisterns are still widely used, if the sanitary fixture you are about to remove is one of these specific categories, you can proceed directly with the next steps, skipping this step.

If, on the other hand, your toilet is equipped with a water cistern, this is the first piece you will remove, starting with the screws and proceeding with great caution, to prevent something from going wrong (and this piece from getting out of hand).

Step 9- Remove the screw caps from the floor.

This is the first actual step in which you are approaching the toilet installation. To begin, remove the screw cap, trying to make sure you remove all of them, in order to proceed more quickly during the next step.

Step 10 - Unscrew the bolts with a wrench.

After removing the outer covering of the bolts, use a wrench (or the one that best suits the shape of the bolts used to hold your old toilet in place) to definitively remove the welding elements that keep this one anchored to the floor. sanitary.

Step 11 - Remove the toilet from its position.

In this toilet assembly phase, you will have to take care of making the toilet detach from the floor, which should also have been welded with silicone. After making sure again that you have removed any screws and removable fastening sources from the toilet bowl, remove the sanitary fixture to be replaced by making slow and controlled forward and backward movements, to gently detach the toilet bowl also from the silicone layer present.

This operation may take longer than the previous ones. Perform each step without rushing and try to speed up the processes.

Step 12 - Remove silicone residue from the floor.

After removing the toilet, you will need to thoroughly clean the entire section of floor that was once underneath the old toilet. Silicone incrustation is not a type of dirt that can be removed with a damp cloth; therefore, it is preferable to have spatulas and metal utensils with which you can scrape off the layer of material stuck to the floor. Be careful to carry out this step delicately, or you risk finding yourself with a silicone-free, but damaged floor.

Guide on how to install a toilet: installation steps

We are finally in the actual toilet installation phase, in which you can finally forget about your old sanitary ware and dedicate hours of your work to furnishing your bathroom with the furnishing elements you have chosen and can't wait to start using.

Step 1 - Cover the drain hole to prevent fumes and bad smells from escaping.

This step is purely of a precautionary nature and is not essential for knowing how to mount a toilet. In the event that you do not want to breathe the smells and fumes coming from the drain hole, immediately after having definitively removed the old sanitary ware, it is preferable to cover this cavity with a medium-thick damp cloth, to avoid that, during all the procedures necessary for the installation and assembly of the toilet, fumes and above all the bad smell that distinguishes these pipes may come out.

Step 2 - Replace the old flange from the exhaust pipe.

Unscrew the old flange, using the special unscrewing keys, and then try to position and fix the new one.

Step 3 - Fit toilet flush to the ground: the gasket.

Start experimenting with the new O-ring to find the perfect fit for this tool. You may have to purchase the gasket separately. There are two types of gaskets:

1. Funnel seal: this is a type of seal that you may need if the attachment of your toilet significantly exceeds the size of the drain cavity. If the dimensions of the exhaust pipe should match, we suggest that you consider the second type of gasket.

2. Flat gasket: it is the type of gasket that minimizes the possibility of obstruction of the drain hole, given its shape that adapts perfectly to the surface, ensuring perfect adherence to the drain cavity.

Regardless of which gasket you choose, make sure that the flange adheres perfectly to the floor, even if this will require several attempts before achieving the expected result. After finding the perfect position, fix the flange by fastening the appropriate screws, including the anchoring ones, essential for correctly positioning and fixing your new toilet.

Step 4 - Install floor toilet on anchor screws.

Lift the toilet bowl onto the anchor screws you just screwed in, taking care to position the sanitary service perfectly in the appropriate calls.

This step, which may seem trivial, fast and immediate, is actually a particularly complicated and long step, which you can only consider finished when you get the perfect positioning, which could require several attempts.

Step 5 - Secure the new toilet to the floor.

To complete the toilet installation step, you will need to make the same forward and backward oscillating movements, just like you did to remove the previous toilet, to ensure perfect adherence of the new toilet to the floor.

Step 6 - Tighten the water pan screws.

Again, this is a step that you will only need to perform if the toilet model you have chosen to install is equipped with a water tank. If your new toilet bowl does not have this section, you can skip and avoid going into this step further.

If this is not the case, insert the screws between the pan and the base of the toilet and start screwing them in by hand, gently and slowly. Perform this step with extreme caution, because, if you leave the screws too loose, you risk infiltration and all the problems related to an infiltration; if instead you were to be excessively energetic, you would run the risk of damaging the screws or their attachment, inevitably and irreparably compromising your new toilet bowl.

Step 7 - Insert wedges or shims into the toilet.

One of the final steps of the intermediate toilet installation phase involves inserting elements that allow you to permanently fix the water tank and the upper part of your new sanitary ware and seal some sections. Indeed, small wedges or shims are fundamental elements to ensure that this object is level.

Step 8 - Tighten the toilet bolts very carefully.

We are approaching the final toilet assembly phases. Always starting with your hands, place the toilet bowl fixing screws in the appropriate calls, and then proceed with extreme caution with the wrench, always to ward off any compromises of the product. The screwing movement that you will have to carry out will be first in one direction and then in its opposite, trying to achieve the greatest possible homogeneity.

Step 9 - Insert the decorative caps and secure the water pan.

After fixing the screws of the new toilet. proceed with the application of the decorative caps for the screws and various nuts and bolts, necessary both to improve the aesthetic result of this piece of furniture and to protect these small but fundamental elements from bad weather, any corrosive substances, accidental falls of objects, etc. After that, you will have to proceed with the definitive fixing of the water tank, making sure that also in this case this fits perfectly with the attachment of the pipes and with the hooks of the toilet itself.

Step 10 - Reconnect the water pipes.

This is the last effective phase you need to know how to assemble a toilet completely and in total autonomy.

After having fixed and welded all the parts that make up this sanitary fixture, you will have to take care of connecting it to the water pipes, reopening the terrestrial key of your home.

Installing a new sink

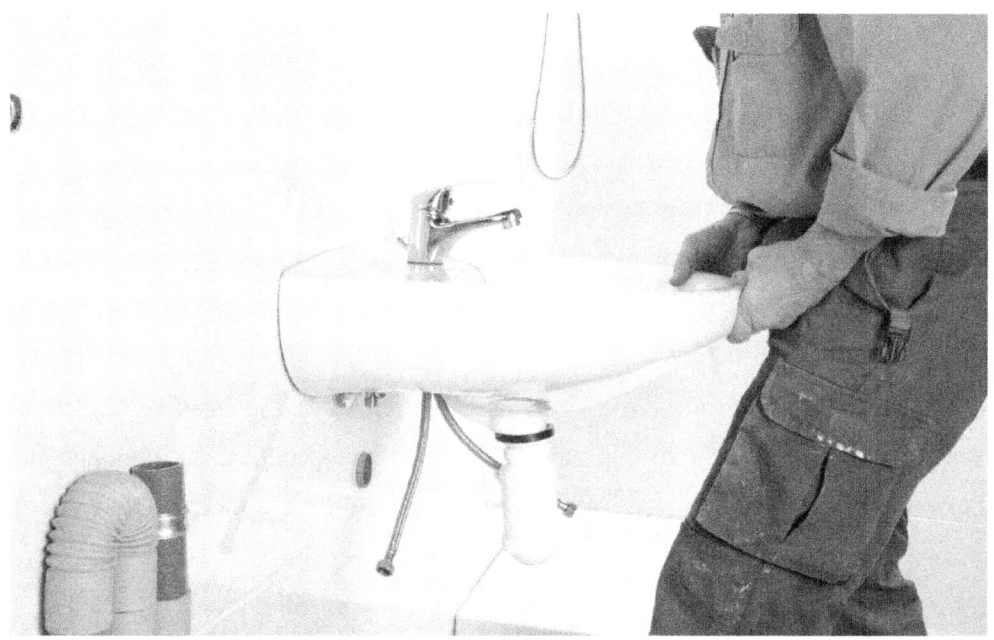

Step 1 - Preparation before assembly: take the measurements and close the central tap.

Before purchasing, take all the measurements: total width of the sink, fixing distance, distance between the drain and the inflow, distance between the floor and the upper corner of the support surface.

Remember: before starting to assemble the sink, empty the pipes and turn off the central tap. Also close the corner valves under the sink.

The siphon of the old sink is disassembled.

Step 2 - Unscrew the siphon and tap from the old sink.

First unscrew the siphon and the water drain hose. Collect the remaining water in a plastic basin. Finally, remove the connections to the faucets under the sink and disassemble the faucets.

Alternative: You can also remove the faucet after unplugging the sink.

Step 3 - Remove the old sink.

Remove the fixing screws present and remove the sink. If the distance or fixing height of the new sink will no longer be the same as before, remove all the fixing material: unscrew the old studs from the wall.

Handyman checks with a spirit level that the holes made with the drill are level.

Step 4 - Drill the holes for the studs.

If you need to drill holes in the tiles, first measure the height at which to fix the new sink.

The height between the upper edge of the sink should be approximately 33.46 inches. The relief should be in the center of the subsequent holes.

Make a sketch to make it easier for you to mount it on the wall. Check the alignment of the holes with the aid of the spirit level.

If you have to drill holes in the tiles, we recommend applying masking tape to prevent the drill from slipping. Drill the holes at the marked points using a tile drill bit. Never use a hammer drill. After drilling through the tiles, use the drill again to drill through the wall, being careful not to damage the tiles. Then apply the appropriate dowels in the holes in the wall and check the stability. The studs are screwed into the wall with a stud driver.

Step 5 - Screw the studs into the wall.

Screw the new studs with a wrench or pliers into the drilled holes until the metric thread protrudes from the wall.

Step 6 - Attach the faucet to the sink.

Insert the new faucet into the holes in the new sink and screw from underneath. Tip: insert the fittings before proceeding with the installation of the sink and do not forget to insert all the gaskets. (For fittings, always observe the manufacturer's instructions!)

For the connection of an electric boiler, a low-pressure coil with 3 connection pipes is required.

Step 7 - Attach the new sink.

Attach the new sink to the protruding portion of the screws so that it remains well supported.

To compensate for any unevenness in the wall and to avoid tensile stresses, apply a strip of sealing mastic to the rear, e.g., with sanitary silicone.

To do this, ask for someone to help you push the sink onto the studs. Do not overtighten the fasteners, this way you can check the position of the sink with a spirit level and correct if necessary. Carry out any corrections in position, symmetrically and so as not to form pressure. Finally, screw the correct retaining clips onto the ends of the studs.

Angle valves are wrapped with Teflon tape.

Step 8 - Insulate the faucets under the sink.

Coat the thread of the new under sink faucets with insulation paste and wrap it in hemp cloth. Alternatively, use Teflon tape. Finally, turn the taps up.

Step 9 - Connect the hoses to the faucets under the sink.

Insert the hose into the faucet under the sink and tighten the union nuts.

Step 10 - Insert the drain.

Insert the drain into the sink opening. Hold the bottom of the valve by pushing it from the bottom and then pulling from the top, then screw it on. Observe the manufacturer's instructions and installation instructions.

The drain hose is inserted into the hole in the wall and connected to the sink.

Step 11 - Insert the exhaust pipe and assemble the exhaust equipment.

Insert the metal drain hose into the hole in the wall. To insulate, use a rubber sleeve. Then mount the exhaust kit and the exhaust valve. Orient the siphon housing opening towards the wall. Fit and install the siphon holders.

Also check the manufacturer's instructions.

Handyman seals the space among the sink and the wall with sanitary silicone.

Step 12 - Seal the space between the sink and the wall

Finally, seal the space between the sink and the wall with sanitary silicone. Observe the manufacturer's instructions and instructions. To spread the silicone, use a silicone scraper dipped in water and detergent.

Here is your new sink, installed quickly and easily. Turn on the water and verify for any leaks. Also check the gasket under the exhaust structure. Your new sink is not only practical and functional, but it also adds that extra touch to your bathroom.

Upgrading your water heater

Now, we will see how to upgrade your water heater. Upgrading your water heater is a common plumbing improvement that can provide many benefits. Here are some things to remind when upgrading your water heater:

1. Type of Water Heater: you can find different water heaters kinds, such us traditional storage tank water heaters, water heaters, tankless and hybrid heat pump water heaters. Each kind has its own pros and cons, so it's vital to opt for the one that best meets your requirements and budget.
2. Size of Water Heater: it's up to on the number of people in your household, your hot water usage habits, and the type of water heater you choose.
3. Energy Efficiency: Upgrading to a more energy-efficient water heater can save you money on your energy bills over time.
4. Installation: Installing a new water heater can be a complex process where knowledge and expertise are needed.
5. Maintenance: Regular check of your water heater can be useful for extending its lifespan and avoid noise costly repairs.
6. Overall, upgrading your water heater can improve your home's energy efficiency, provide more reliable hot water, and save you money in the long run.

As last advice, we want you to remember to choose the right water heater for your home and ensure that it is installed and maintained correctly.

Step-by-step projects

We close the chapter with the creation of a do-it-yourself plumbing projects, taking up some things already said and indicating some new ones.

1. Replace a leaky faucet

We've already seen how to replace a faucet. Let's see in detail:
- ✓ Close the general tap that feeds the mixer.
- ✓ Disassemble the old mixer by unscrewing the fixing nut from under the sink.
- ✓ Remove the joints of the hot and cold-water pipes.
- ✓ Clean the surface gently with a spatula to remove the traces of limescale that form around the mixer.
- ✓ Keep on reassembling the new mixer.

2. Fix a running toilet

The toilet first fixing operation, if you have followed the previous toilet installation guide to the end, at this this points you have already done it and consists in using screws and bolts to allow the toilet to adhere perfectly to the flooring. To seal the toilet to the floor, which is a complementary but not equal step to fixing, you will need silicone to definitively seal your new piece of furniture to the floor, completely installed and ready to be used. Anyway, see again the previous paragraph "how to install a new toilet".

3. Install a new showerhead

List of needs

- ✓ Your new shower head, keep it close at hand.
- ✓ A rag or soft cloth to protect the finish of the shower head.
- ✓ Cleaning material, such as an old toothbrush or paper towel.
- ✓ An adjustable spanner and possibly also pliers.
- ✓ Sealing tape.

How to proper install the showerhead

1. **Turn off the faucet**. To avoid flooding the bathroom, before disassembling the old shower head, make sure the tap is turned off! Unlike when you have to replace the sink faucet, you don't have to turn off the water valve as well.

2. **Spread a tarp**. While this step may seem unnecessary to some, it is a good way to prevent damage and wasted materials. That way nothing will go down the drain accidentally. In addition, you will also protect the bathtub or shower tray in case some tools are dropped.

3. **Unscrew your existing shower head**. A seemingly simple enough operation at best. Unscrew the shower head making sure not to damage it. If the shower head resists, use the adjustable wrench to turn it gently and with a pair of pliers hold the tube in place, being careful not to damage either by using a soft cloth. You'll see, it will be easy!

4. **Give everything a good clean**. The shower arm may have some old grime buildup. Give it a good scrub with the toothbrush or clean it with paper towels if there is not too much dirt. Make sure you don't damage the arm ferrule!

5. **Start taping by applying masking tape to the thread of your new shower head.** Start at the bottom, wrap the tenderloin all the way around and continue to the end. Press the tape into the grooves of the thread.

Practical tip: make sure you apply the tape in a clockwise direction! If you wind it counterclockwise you run the risk of damaging or unraveling the tape once you screw the new head onto the shower.

6. **Away with the old... and welcome the new!** Now you can attach your new shower head. To screw in (clockwise) the new shower head you probably won't need any tools and can simply do it by hand.

7. **Open the faucet.** Make sure the shower head is facing you and turn on the faucet to let some water flow. If you notice any leaks, stop the flow immediately and check that you have screwed the new shower head all the way in. Otherwise, you're done.

4. **Replace a toilet flange**

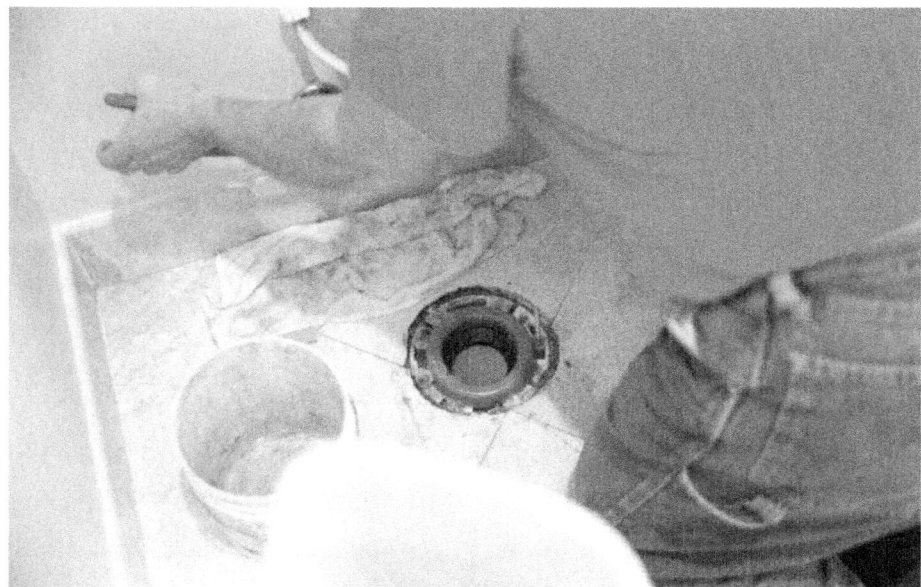

Water at the bottom is one of the most common signs of a bad toilet flange. It is difficult to replace a toilet flange, as it is not like other toilet parts. This is because it sits at the base of the toilet, which means you'll have to take the entire toilet apart to replace it.

The toilet flange connects the toilet base with the waste pipe in the bathroom floor. The flange is circular and is where the wax ring is located. It is also known as a cabinet-flange. As stated earlier, removing or replacing a toilet flange is quite challenging. The rest is simple once the toilet is removed.

Water leaking from the base of the toilet is an indication that the flange needs to be checked. Also, if the toilet rocks back and forth during use, the flange is probably broken. The process is very simple and there is no need to call a plumber. Also, make sure you get the right plunger before replacing the damaged one. Here's how to replace a toilet flange.

Step 1: Get the right tools.

If you're preparing to remove an old or damaged flange, you'll need a few tools to help you carry out the toilet repair. These include an adjustable wrench, rubber gloves, old rag, multi head screwdriver, nose and mouth mask, tape measure, putty knife, newspaper, hacksaw and the right bolts and screws for attaching a flange.

Step 2: Shut off the water supply.

When you have all the tools mentioned above, you can go ahead and replace the flange. Turn off the water supply to your bathroom. The toilet shutoff valve is usually located behind the toilet from the floor or wall behind it.

To stop the water flow, turn the valve clockwise and disconnect the water supply line.

Step 3: Clean the bathroom.

Once the water supply is disconnected, flush the toilet to remove any water left in the tank or bowl. You can repeat the wash until no more water is drained. Use a sponge, towel or vacuum cleaner, for removing any water residue in the bowl and tank. You will be able to work in a dry area as water can splash out of the tank as you move it.

Step 4: Take out the dice.

Now that you've disconnected the water supply line and tank, it's time to take out the toilet seat. To accomplish this, you'll need to remove the nuts holding the toilet to the ground. Two dice are usually found on most toilets, one on each side. Some toilets have plastic caps that need to be removed before the bolts can be unscrewed. You can remove the bolts with a hacksaw if they're hard to reach.

Step 5: remove the toilet and set it aside.

You can lift the toilet yourself or ask someone to help you, depending on the kind of toilet. Put newspapers or rags everywhere you're going to put the toilet. The toilet can be gently lifted from its place and placed on the newspaper. You should lift the toilet until it is free of the bolts. You should hold some water in the toilet while you lift it. A rag is a good idea for cleaning the bathroom.

Step 6: Cover the outflow pipe with a cloth.

After lifting the toilet from its base, you should close the sewer hole/waste pipe to prevent a bad smell from filling your bathroom. Use a cloth or rag large enough to close the hole. Don't wait to remove the old flange before plugging the hole, as the smell in the bathroom will become unbearable.

Step 7: clean the flange.

Next, clean and monitor the toilet flange. Start by removing the old wax ring using a putty knife.. You may find a worn or deformed wax ring. Also, it will be sticky as you remove it. Continue removing the wax ring with the knife.

If the flange is in bad condition, remove it and throw it away. But if it's in good shape, clean the wax ring, wipe it clean, and put a new wax ring in the toilet before reinstalling it.

Step 8: remove the flange.

However, if the wax ring is in a terrible state, get rid of it. The bolts that secure the toilet flange to the floor must be removed. There are usually four. Turn them counterclockwise with the help of a screwdriver to remove them. Even though the new toilet flange comes with its own screws, you should only keep the old screws as spares if you need them.

Remove the flange and place it on a newspaper or rag before disposing of it later. Toilet flanges are usually made of PVC and sealed by a gasket. Unlike toilet flanges made from PVC, these are easy to remove but fixed to a PVC waste pipe or a cast iron flange integrated into the cast iron waste pipe.

Step 9: acquire the correct toilet flange.

Now it's time to replace the toilet flange. The most common error people make is purchasing the wrong size toilet flange.

Since there are different types and sizes of toilet flanges, it is crucial that you buy the right one. The most common toilet flange has a diameter of 3.9 inches. It is essential to measure your existing flange to determine the right flange for your toilet. You can take the old flange with you to get the correct replacement. You can find the required toilet flange size at your local hardware store.

Step 10: install new flange and wax ring.

Toilet flange manufacturers offer a new flange with a new wax band. If your flange doesn't have a wax ring, it's worth buying one. Install the flange and then the wax ring. Make sure all bolts and screws are securely in place to ensure the toilet does not move after installation.

Step 11: Reinstall the Toilette.

After installing the flange and placing the wax ring on the toilet, remove the rag or cloth in the waste pipe. Next, reinstall the toilet. Do this carefully because you don't want to drop the toilet. Tighten the nuts by hand before tightening them with a wrench, as overtightening the nuts could crack the toilet. Then adjust the water level in the bowl correctly. Make sure the toilet is placed directly on the flange. Once the toilet is in place, apply some pressure near the back of the rim of the bowl to deform the wax and form an excellent wax seal.

Finally, tighten the bolts to the base of the toilet and reconnect the water supply. Allow the toilet tank to fill by opening the flush valve.

Step 12: check the bathroom.

Test the toilet after filling it. There should be no water leaks on the bathroom floor. Repair the water leak if it leaks. Your job is done and there is no need to replace the toilet. Now you can enjoy your toilet and bathroom without any worries.

5. Fix a clogged sink

If you have a clogged sink, there are several things you can do to fix the problem:

- ✓ Try a suction cup unclog: Insert the suction cup into the sink, making sure it is completely covered by water. Next, press down on the suction cup and then pull up in a vigorous motion to create negative pressure and force the water to push the plug into the tube.
- ✓ Use a chemical blockage remover: You can purchase a chemical blockage remover at any hardware store or supermarket. Pour the product into the sink, follow the instructions on the package and wait for the indicated time. Then, rinse with warm water to remove the product and see if the obstruction has been cleared.
- ✓ Use a pipe snake: If the suction cup and chemical blockage remover aren't working, you may need to use a pipe snake.

6. Replace a damaged pipe

The pipes that transport and distribute cold and domestic hot water, but also those of heating systems, especially the traditional metal types, are subject to wear and tear and accidental breakage which can compromise their seal and integrity.

The main damages due to wear and tear are linked to limescale deposits and rusting of the pipes, more frequent in old houses.

Sometimes it can also happen that you accidentally drill or crack a walled-in pipe, simply by making holes with a drill or other tools, during small housework, causing water to leak.

In traditional constructions they are almost always walled inside the plastered or tiled walls of the bathroom and kitchen, or they run inside the attics finished with the flooring.

Therefore, they can never be inspected: the damaged pipe is only visible when there are more or less visible water leaks, with the formation of stains and flooding.

As a rule, to avoid nasty surprises, it is better to completely replace a water system after 20/25 years and rely on expert technicians, but it is also possible to do it yourself.

Emergency repair of a pipe

In the face of a sudden loss of water it is possible to put in place temporary remedies to seal holes and cracks.

It must be considered that it is a buffer solution that can serve for a few hours, during which it is better to keep the taps tightly closed.

The most common products consist of sealing pastes and bandages.

For pipes made of plastic material, metals and composite materials, for example, it is possible to use bandages of glass fibers impregnated with polyurethane glue which harden in contact with water in about 30 minutes.

Replace the pipe

To remedy a broken pipe that leaks water, it is always necessary to break the wall and replace the entire section involved, from joint to joint.

However, it is necessary to carefully evaluate the intervention from time to time: in fact, if the system is old and already worn out, it is more convenient to remove it and make a completely new one.

The most used pipes for the home water system are made of PVC with a diameter of 1.56 inches, often chosen also because they are rather cheap.

Among the most recent on the market those in heat-shrinking plastic material, with a chemical composition that makes them resistant to limescale and corrosion.

7. **Install a new water filtration system**

Home water filtration and purification systems are increasingly popular because they solve two very common problems such as the need to improve the quality of tap water — for drinking, for washing food or dishes or for cooking — and at the same time the easiest way to say goodbye to bulky, uncomfortable and polluting plastic bottles and do the planet a favor.

The filtration category that interests us is that of purification systems to be applied directly on the tap, so as to treat the water through a filter before dispensing it at various intensities; installation is pretty simple, as is maintenance — as long as you just replace the filters when they reach the end of their life. To do this you need the so-called under-sink filters which are easy to install.

To install an under-sink system, first of all it is necessary to divert the cold water so as to have the water intake for both the unfiltered cold water and the filtered cold water.

Once the cold-water deviation has been created with the appropriate Tee fitting with stop closure, it is possible to create the water line with pipes for food use. Quick connections allow the hose to be engaged from the stop closure to the filter inlet. In this regard, we must know that each filter has its own head, and that the cartridge must be inserted into the head equipped with a bayonet connection.

The heads always have quick couplings and an obligatory direction for both the inlet and outlet of the water, so it is very important to check the arrow that indicates the water flow.

Once the pipe entering and exiting the head has been connected, the next step is to put together the pipe to our tap.

In this regard, we can use two different types of faucet:
- ✓ 1-way tap
- ✓ 3-way faucet

The 1-way taps require an additional hole on the sink and are dedicated to the supply of filtered water only. It is therefore associated with a classic 2-way tap for dispensing hot and cold water.

The 3-way taps, on the other hand, allow you to have a single dispensing point without having to make a second hole in the sink. From the same tap it is, therefore, possible to dispense hot and cold water or filtered water. Inside the 3-way taps the filtered water channel is entirely separated from the channel dedicated to hot and cold water to avoid any type of contamination.

Whatever the choice of filter, having an under-sink system allows you to drink tap water in complete safety with considerable family savings.

8. Add a new outdoor faucet

If you have a garden, it can be handy to have an outdoor faucet. This makes it easier for you to water your flowers and plants or wash your windows or car.

Step 1 - Pipe freezing prevention.

Mount the outside faucet about 19,6 inches above the ground. Don't forget to empty the pipe in the winter to prevent freezing. This means that the faucet must be higher than where you connect the hose. Then you can fit a drain cock at the bottom of the pipe. Of course, it is helpful for the new pipe to be as short as possible to minimize the risk of freezing.

Step 2 - Water supply

The main water shutoff valve pipe usually has a large diameter. Branches of this pipe are usually 15mm in diameter and some of the pipes at points of use may be 0.47 inches in diameter. Therefore, you have to operate with pipes of various diameters.

Step 3 - Find the right position.

Select where you want to mount the faucet and where the pipe should go through the wall. Drill a 0.78 inches hole through the wall from the inside out. You can mount the faucet on a wall plate or with a countersunk wall mount. Insert part of the electrical conduit tubing through the hole and fill any gaps with sealant. You can bend the pipes yourself or you can use elbow fittings. We recommend the use of compression fittings for their convenience.

Step 4 - Close the main shut-off valve.

Before starting work, you should close the main shut-off valve. Open all supply valves and let the pipes drain.

Step 5 - Cut the feed tube.

Locate where you want to insert the tee into the inlet hose to connect to the outside faucet. Then cut the feed tube with a hacksaw or pipe cutter and remove approximately 0.78 inches of length from the tube. File away imperfections and smooth the pipe ends with wet and dry sandpaper. If the workspace on the pipe is limited, you can use a grinder. If so, be sure to wear safety glasses.

Step 6 - Compression fittings.

These fittings could be found in all shapes and sizes: with different diameters and as adapters, tees, elbows and end fittings. To assemble the tee, slide the nut followed by the washer or compression ring along one end of the pipe. Then insert the tee onto the end of the pipe and carefully push the compression ring towards the tee. Make sure the nut fits straight in and rotates smoothly. Then slide the nut and compression ring down the other end of the hose, insert it into the tee, and tighten the nut by hand until it is snug.

Step 7 - Tighten securely.

Finally, tighten the nuts securely with an appropriately sized wrench or an adjustable wrench. Tighten carefully, as copper is soft and easily damaged. One turn of the nut is usually sufficient to ensure a watertight seal.

Step 8 -The drain cock.

Place the pipe with any elbow and compression fittings up to the hole in the outside wall. Install a drain cock at the bottom of the pipe so that you can drain the pipe in freezing weather. Secure the pipe to the walls with pipe stops or brackets, using at least 1 stop or bracket for every meter of pipe.

Step 9 - Mount the wall plate.

Drill mounting holes in the wall, insert the wall plugs and screw the plate in place. Connect the tubing to the fitting in the plate and secure everything tightly. Use a faucet with an aerator. This is a particular valve placed into the faucet that prevents vacuums from forming if the water pressure drops.

Step 10 - Countersunk mounting bracket.

Put a plate you can use a countersunk wall mount, with the faucet partially recessed into the wall. This makes it less vulnerable and gives a very professional looking result. Make the countersunk mount fixed into the wall with quick-setting cement. This hardens within 20 minutes. Wrap PTFE tape around the faucet thread and mount the faucet securely onto the flared mounting bracket. Open the main shutoff valve and check for leaks.

9. Replace a bathtub drain

The bathtubs are designed to have an anti-overflow drainage system and there are two types: the first is a filler, or a system where the overflow must be connected first and then the siphon; the second is a siphon, where the plastic tube connects to the siphon itself.

In the case of the union type, the union must be fixed to its inlet and the grate inserted on the drain from inside the tub. From below, add the plastic (or rubber) gasket and tighten the retaining nut. Add some silicone sealant to prevent leaks.

Install the slide between the tub siphon and the drain spout. Wrap Teflon tape around the drain hose connection for extra security.

10. Install a new garbage disposal

There are many different types of garbage disposal units on the market, but the basics of garbage disposal plumbing are the same. Whether it's starting a new installation, replacing an older model, or simply repairing plumbing lines, once you understand the basics, the task will be done the same no matter what the situation demands.

When installing a new unit, the garbage disposal plumbing must be set up correctly for it to function properly, without blocking the main drain lines. The first step is to remove all of the old piping from under the sink and then connect the new ones to the bottom drain hole in the sink, making sure the garbage disposal drain line is pointing toward the main drain's exit point. Downward angled pipe should be installed from the unit and then a trap at the bottom of the run. After the trap, the pipes will rise and connect to the main drain line, connecting to the pipe coming from the second half of the sink, if any. This design allows waste piping to be separated from the rest of the plumbing lines in case plugging or repairs need to be done.

When replacing a garbage disposal, the first step will be to remove the existing waste pipes and then remove them from the bottom of the sink. The old drive is then removed and the new one is put in place. The new item will then be sealed to the outer ring of the drain coming from the sink and the plumbing lines linked to it, substituting any parts and fittings as required. This process is basically the same as when installing a new unit, but the garbage disposal plumbing usually doesn't need to be removed and replaced.

Repairing a garbage disposal begins in much the same way as replacing the unit. If the disposal is to be removed and rebuilt, the plumbing lines will need to be disconnected from it, as well as removing it from the sink. If it just leaks, the section responsible for the problem can simply be replaced. One of the most basic concepts of garbage disposal plumbing is making sure that all connections are sealed properly and that any cracked or broken pieces are replaced as soon as they are noticed.

The basics of garbage disposal plumbing is simply a process of knowing how drain lines work and why separate traps are installed. In order to maximize unit efficiency while reducing the chances of pipe blockage, waste disposal drain lines should be kept separate from main drains until a trap is installed. This allows easy access to clear blockages that the unit may be causing, preventing them from backing up the entire plumbing system.

Having finished explaining you how to do your own DIY plumbing, in the next section we will explain how to do the electrical one.

PART 4: Electrical

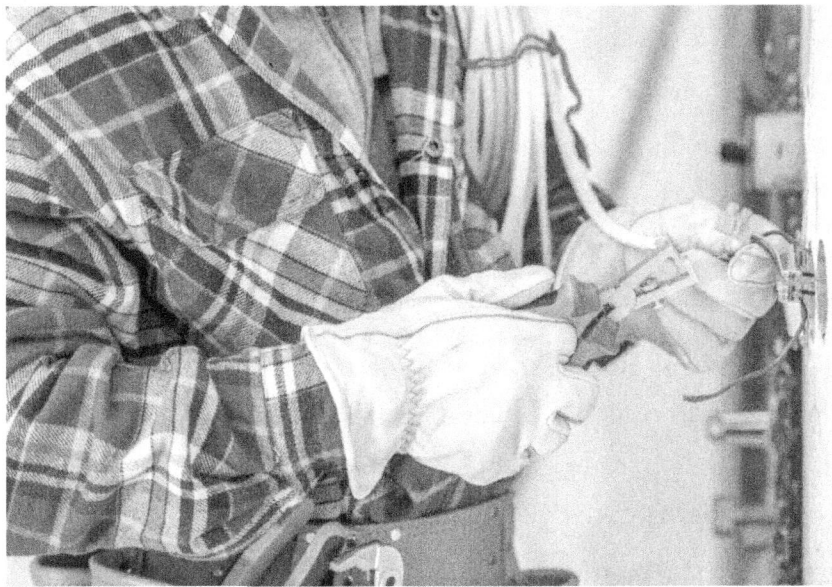

This chapter covers basic electrical tasks such as substituting light switches and outlets, as well as more advanced tasks like installing ceiling fans and whole-house surge protectors.

Basic electrical repairs

Again, let's start with the basics of the electrical system repairs. When renovating an apartment, little attention is usually paid to the electrical system: often the new inhabitants do not have clear ideas on exactly how they will furnish the new home and, consequently, on where to position the electrical outlets and switches. This makes it necessary to resort to subsequent interventions and modifications, with a consequent and not negligible increase in costs. The inconvenience due to a late design of the electrical system can be avoided by acting promptly, before starting the renovations. No special planning is required for simple installations. Below we will provide you a brief guide to intervene on the electrical system of the house and repair the most frequent faults quickly and easily, but above all in total safety.

<u>Secure electrical connections</u>

When connecting electrical wires to an appliance or device, you may have difficulty locking the wires into their terminals.
In this case, apply a drop of hot glue to each connection. Its insulating power guarantees the safety of the connection, and its adhesion strength ensures its stability.

Water repellent protection

There is a way to insulate electrical connections exposed to the elements from water or humidity. Dissolve a certain amount of packing polystyrene in a nitro solvent. Appropriately dose the components to obtain a more or less thick compound according to the use you intend to make of them: a thick compound poured on the connections effectively protects them from humidity and wetness.

Clogged hose

It is not uncommon for pieces of mortar or foreign material to fall into the electrical boxes and block the hose. In this case, inserting the cables becomes impossible. To fix it without having to break the wall, blow from the opposite end, using a piece of pipe of a suitable diameter as a connection between the box and the mouth or the compressor.

Conductor interrupted

Appliance cords can break in nowhere due to the intense wear and tear to which they are subjected. Locating the exact point of the break with the tester allows you not to cut pieces of cable unnecessarily and saves a lot of time. Insert pins in different points of the cable, and by touching them with the tester, look for the exact point of the interruption. Cut this section of cable and make a junction using insulated connectors.

Prepare the ends of the electrical wires

For preparing the leads of the electrical wires quickly and accurately, first cut the plastic insulating coating.
Instead of pulling the piece off, as is usually done, twist it between your fingers so that the copper braid rolls up tightly.
Remove the sheath continuing the rotation movement: in this way the end of the electric wire will be perfectly compact.

Tin the lugs

When making an electrical system, it is advisable to tin the ends of the wires with a soldering iron to ensure safe contact. If there are few wires this does not involve particular problems, but if the number of wires to be treated is considerable, it is advisable to immerse their ends in molten tin in a saucepan placed on a stove.

Repair circuit boards

To restore parts of circuit boards that have suffered damage, you can use the foil coating of chocolate packaging or paper to preserve food. Shape the material to restore the electronic connections and secure it with cyanoacrylate glue. Be careful how you use this glue because, being an insulator, its incorrect use can compromise the functionality of the circuit.

Use the phase finder

Repairing the electrical system with the phase finder the phase finder has the external appearance of a screwdriver. The transparent handle holds a small neon bulb.

Touching the electric cables or active metal parts of outlets and plugs with the tip of the phase finder, it is ascertained whether the element touched is live or not: if it is live, the light bulb turns on.

It is thus easy to check before starting a job and, once the job is finished, if a given element is live or not, and if it is connected to live wires of the system (phase wires) or to those normally not live (power neutral).

Does the earth work?

To test if the ground of a power cord is connected to the body of an appliance, make a simple electrical circuit with some wires, a battery and a light bulb.

Connect the circuit to the central pin of the plug and to the metal body of the appliance: if the light bulb turns on, the earth connection is active, and the appliance guarantees a certain degree of safety during use.

Calibrate the tester

To properly calibrate the graduated scale of a tester, position the selector on the resistance measurement, bring the two tips into contact and with the adjustment knob make sure that the pointer of the tester points to the maximum value of the graduated scale.

Replacing outlets and switches

Let's see now how to replace outlets and switches.

Replacing electrical outlets: the phases of the work

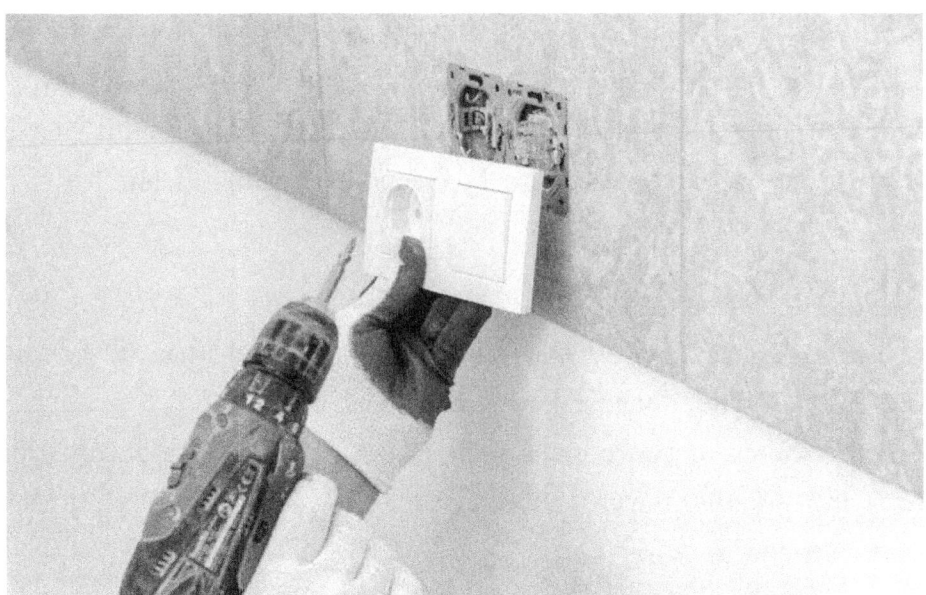

As first step, you should disconnect the power supply:

Disconnect the electricity supply to the house before starting any work on the system. Simply lower the switch lever located on the meter or on the circuit breaker.

Step 2 - Remove the cover plate.

Remove the cover plate from the electrical box, usually a snap-fit one, levering slightly with a screwdriver on the back of the same plate. For other types of plates, the screws are unscrewed, where present. In both cases you should pay attention to don't damage the visible part of the cover plate.

Step 3 - Unscrew the metal support.

Inside the box, the metal support on which the plug of the electrical socket is located, i.e. the device that allows you to use the electric current at the point in which it is located, must be unscrewed.

Step 4 - Unscrew the electrical wires from the fruit.

The electrical cables must be unscrewed from the fruit, which are normally: the brown phase, the blue neutral and the yellow-green earth. Check the section of the cables, which must not be less than 3,2 square feet, otherwise they will need to be replaced. A cable section of less than 3.2 square feet jeopardizes the safety and efficiency of the system, because cables with an unsuitable section could heat up excessively when passed through by electric current. replacement of electrical outlets

Step 5 - Remove the portion of the covering sheath.

With the electrician's scissors, remove the portion of the covering sheath and highlight the internal copper conductors. According to the standard, the phase and neutral conductors must be screwed respectively into the upper and lower terminal of the insert of the new socket, while the yellow-green conductor must be connected to the central terminal of the same. cut the electric cable

Step 6 - Reinstall the plate in the cassette.

Check the correct connection and reinstall the plate in the cassette. Lastly, reapply the finishing mask. Change the electrical outlet.

Step 7 - Test the operation of the socket.

At the end of the work, lift the lever of the system switch again and test the operation of the socket.

Step 8 - Add a fruit.

In an already installed box, it is possible to add a new fruit, if prearranged. Remove the grip plate and remove the fake spacer insert. Move the already present inserts, so that they are placed side by side, to install the new insert in a lateral position and facilitate the insertion of the power supply jumpers, created using sections of insulated electric cable. After verifying the correct connection, proceed with the phases of fixing the plate and restoring the current.

Replace switches

Replacing a light switch is certainly not part of the normal routine. Nonetheless, the work may become necessary if there is deterioration and consequent switch malfunction, as well as in the event of an interrupted light point, or during modernization or restyling works, of the electrical system in general.

In any case, replacing the power switch is a fairly simple operation, so much so that it can even be carried out in self-made mode, provided you strictly comply with the mandatory safety standards. The type of electric switch found most frequently in homes is that of the so-called unipolar switch to which reference will be made below, for the relative removal and subsequent assembly phases.

Light switch replacement

The bipolar switch operation provides that the interruption of the electric flow takes place both on the phase and on the neutral, i.e. on the two poles. Normally all the protection switches in the electrical panel of a building are bipolar; it must be understood that, for the correct maintenance of the latter more demanding and delicate devices, it is absolutely advisable to have the intervention of authorized technical personnel.

Before even preparing to replace the current switch yourself, you need to get a switch of the same brand and model as the one to be changed: it will be available in any electrical component shop, or even in large retailers, at a competitive price.

If you wish to change gender, especially as regards the aesthetic layout, your trusted dealer will certainly be able to advise which switches can be well suited to the specific case.

The necessary tools are only flathead and star screwdrivers of the appropriate size and a special tester to verify the absence of voltage on the circuit on which you are going to work. Then just follow the few simple steps below and the job will be completed correctly.

Removing plate and electric switch

For the purposes of your own safety and that of others, it should be remembered that it is absolutely essential first of all to ensure that the main switch is correctly closed.

Before starting any type of intervention, as in all cases in which one works on electrical systems, it is necessary to disconnect the main switch of the current, to operate on the electrical system in absolute safety.

If you are not entirely sure that you have cut off the electricity supply to the home system, it is preferable rather to avoid proceeding with the work.

Light switch replacement

Before being able to access the switch, the old metal or plastic plate that covers the switch support itself must be removed. The plate can be fixed to the support in two ways:

- ✓ With two screws, by unscrewing which it is possible to detach the plate.
- ✓ Securing the plate to the support with an interlocking system whereby, to remove it, it will be necessary to lever with a slotted screwdriver, below the plate in the appropriate release opening.

We then proceed with the removal of the support and the switch

The support, which can be seen once the plate has been removed, is fixed to the electrical box by means of two screws which can generally be removed with both star and slotted screwdrivers.

Once the screws are removed, the bracket with the switch attached will easily come away from the wall exposing the electrical circuit wires.

If you have a digital tester or even a more common phase tester screwdriver, you can check that the circuit is not live, if you are not completely sure that you have previously disconnected the electrical system.

If the circuit is still powered, it is absolutely necessary to avoid going ahead with the work and be sure to disconnect the electrical system in complete safety.

At this point, the broken switch must be detached from the support

Usually, the current switch is fixed with an interlocking system and can be easily released by levering with a slotted screwdriver between the switch itself and the support.

Once the switch has been released, all that remains is to disconnect the wires by unscrewing the screws on the switch with a Phillips or slotted screwdriver.

Wiring a new circuit or outlet

Here you are some recommendations for the correct assembly and wiring of the new current switch
Let's see how to proceed with the assembly of the new switch, in complete safety.

The wires, previously disconnected from the failed switch, can be connected to the new switch. There are usually three holes, clearly visible on the switch; the important thing is that one of the wires is inserted into the central hole.

Replace the light switch: move the wires

Once the wires have been inserted into the holes, tighten the clamp screws firmly to lock the wires firmly in place. Once the wires are screwed in, the new switch must be fitted into the support making sure that the tab has snapped in properly, otherwise you risk seeing the switch go back into the wall when you then turn on the light.

Subsequently, the support can be screwed onto the switch box, taking care to fold the wires back to the back of the switch. If the wires should hinder the support resting on the box, it means that they have not been folded in the most appropriate way.

In this case, it is not necessary to force the support on the cassette in order not to risk irreversibly damaging the wires but on the contrary, it is necessary to find a more suitable position, which allows the support to be screwed easily.

Fitting new light switch

Once the support has been fixed to the wall, the plate will have to be reassembled which, depending on the case, will be fitted or screwed onto the support. At this point, all that remains is to verify the correctness of the work performed. The circuit breaker will then be flipped up to restore power to the circuit.

By turning on the light, it will be possible to verify that the new current switch is installed in a workmanlike manner and works perfectly, as well as the rest of the electrical system. If you have experience with electrical work and decide to tackle the project yourself, here are some general steps to follow:

1. Establish the location: Decide where you want to mount the new outlet or circuit and ensure that it is in compliance with local electrical codes.

2. Turn off the power: Before beginning any work, turn off the power to the circuit that you will be working on. This can be done at the circuit breaker panel.
3. Run the cable from the circuit breaker panel to the place of the new outlet or circuit. Be quite sure the cable is the proper size and suitable for the job.
4. Install the outlet or circuit: Install the outlet or circuit according to the manufacturer's instructions and local electrical codes. Be sure to link the wires correctly and securely.
5. Test the circuit: Once the outlet or circuit is installed, turn the power back on and test it with a voltage tester to ensure that it is working properly.

Installing lighting fixtures and ceiling fans

Lighting fixtures are very functional, both for their small size and for their neutral design, which can be combined with any type of environment and furniture. Another good reason to create a lighting system of this type is the luminous flux, which is absolutely satisfactory and economical, thanks to the low energy consumption. Making a small lighting fixture for a study, a room or a closet at home is quite easy, but it will be necessary to have a minimum of experience and skills in the DIY field. But let's see how to proceed to prepare one. Necessary

- ✓ LED or other light bulbs
- ✓ Copper wire
- ✓ Tin welder
- ✓ 12 Volt transformer
- ✓ Resistances.

Connect the two ends of the electric wire

If you need a small fixed led light, it will be sufficient to connect the two ends of the electric wire that pass through a 12 Volt transformer. If you want to create a small multiple light bulbs system for your hi-fi system, perhaps by combining different colors, then you will have to make a connection between the light bulbs and the transformer, through the so-called "parallel connection". This term, in electrical engineering, indicates an identical current intensity for all the involved. Conversely, if you connect single Light bulbs to different transformers, the connection will be defined as "serial".

Pass the paws of each thread from the underside

After this brief digression on the fundamental principles of electrical connections, you will need to get everything you need to build the system that's right for you. You will need to buy the Light bulbs, a good number of resistors (the ones with the colored stripes), a 12 Volt transformer and some wire. First of all, you will have to insert the light bulbs on a plastic plate on which you will have to make small holes with a DIY drill. The holes will accommodate the ends of the electrical wire. At this point, assuming that you have to install 3 light bulbs on the plate, after having passed the paws.

Close the circuit

To obtain the desired result, the scheme must follow a very specific criterion. You will have to start by connecting a resistor, and then proceed with the various connections between the light bulbs, scrupulously respecting the polarities of the terminals. You will then have to close the circuit with another resistor of the same Ohm value as the first. All connections between light bulbs, resistors and copper wires will be held together with tin soldering.

The system is complete, so you just have to connect the electric wire (red and black) to the two ends of the circuit, equip it with pins that will be inserted in the positive and negative polarity of the 12 Volt transformer.

Ceiling fan: how to install it

Ceiling fans, once used only in tropical countries, have gradually conquered even temperate areas thanks to their particular qualities.

The paddle fan pleasantly cools a room without creating strong drafts.

The fan has long ceiling blades that rotate slowly moving a considerable mass of air, without causing excessively intense currents, which could create problems for those who are hit by them, but generating a slight breeze which, helping perspiration in a natural way, offers significant heat relief.

The area affected by the air flow is, on the floor, about twice the diameter of the blades.

Electrical circuit diagram

As can be understood from the fencing we can see in comparison:

- ✓ Diagram of the circuit in which only the multi-speed manual command is foreseen.
- ✓ This component can be replaced by a remote-control receiver.
- ✓ Circuit which foresees the use of a thermostat in combination with the manual control.

The low-speed rotation of the ceiling blades is also extremely silent, and the induction motor produces no noise. It is believed, erroneously, that a fan of this type is only used in the summer, to cool people down.

Instead, it is also very useful in winter, when the heating is on in the house.

In fact, it happens that the heat accumulates in the upper part of the rooms while the lower part is at a lower temperature. A room thermostat, which reads the temperature at a height of 1.5 meters, keeps the system on until the desired temperature is reached.

Ceiling fan in the bedroom

If there is a slowly rotating fan in the room, the heat accumulated at the top is sent downwards, the thermostat detects a higher temperature and will keep the system on for a shorter period, with significant fuel savings.

Installing the ceiling fan

The system is made up of a speed regulator switch placed in an easily accessible point, which sends voltage to a thermostat, installed on the ceiling, which enables the fan to start according to the temperature at which it is set.

The switch can also be kept on permanently, leaving the thermostat to start the fan when certain temperatures are reached.

Naturally, the system can also do without the thermostat and be controlled directly by the multi-speed switch. The model used in these pages is not equipped with a remote control, but the presence of the latter does not change the electrical circuit significantly.

The fan is purchased in kit form and must be assembled before suspending it: the three power cables must be inserted into the support bar and connected to the respective motor terminals, including the earth one since the body of the fan is metal.

When the body of the fan is assembled, you can proceed with the installation of the blades which are inserted into position in the appropriate housings and blocked by means of screws with nuts.

The blades have a particular shape and cannot be mounted upside down. Finally, you can switch to suspension. Generally, it is carried out in the center of the room, suspending the fan from the walled hook of the chandelier. This, among other things, allows you to have the conductors available for its operation even if they will have to be connected in a different way.

Power rod and cables

Here are the elements required for assembly. The body of the fan is purchased disassembled and is assembled upon assembly. The small parts are reduced to a minimum.

Rod and fan power cables at this point, start by inserting the motor power cables inside the hollow suspension bar. The ground wire is also included.

To prevent the rotation of the blades from causing progressive loosening of the nut, insert and widen a locking pin.

General assembly

Insert the three cables coming out from the lower part of the bar into the terminals placed on the upper part of the motor, also the earth cable.

Assembly sequences: in the upper part of the bar, you have to insert a special rubber that is used to create a cushioning effect. The washer must also be blocked by a bolt, stopped with a cotter pin. The suspension hook is inserted into the washer.

Here's what the bar attached to the engine looks like. The domes are gathered in the center for a better view of the structure.

How to install the switch

When the fan is suspended from the ceiling the hoods will be moved to cover the connections. Mount the blades and carry out the suspension.

The cruise control switch should be applied to the wall.

Send a conduit with the necessary cables to the appropriate point.

Fan switch installation sequence. Remove the bottom of the appliance and drill it in the appropriate point so as to be able to let the conductors coming out of the wall pass through. Apply the base to the wall and, keeping it horizontal, mark the fixing holes for inserting the dowels and lock it firmly.

Chandelier placement and thermostat connection

A conflict can arise between the chandelier and the fan, which can be remedied in two different ways: either place alternative lighting elements such as lampshades, spotlights, or use a fan with built-in light or, better still, a ceiling fan with light.

Chandelier fan

It is a particular model of fan chandelier, available in different versions which, under the motor, has a bowl with a light bulb and therefore performs the double task of refreshing and illuminating. In any case, the fan blades must be at least 2.5 meters away from the floor and care must be taken that they cannot be reached via other elements of the house such as elevations, fixed stairs, etc.

Let's move on to connecting the thermostat. Press-fit the central part of the regulator and connect the conductors according to the connection diagrams in the instruction leaflet.

At this point, apply the thermostat to the ceiling and connect it to two of the cables coming from the regulator. Then make the remaining connections as well. At the end, mount the blades in the points indicated and with the correct obligatory inclination.

The electrical connection

In the simplest case, in which you do not intend to use the thermostat, you must apply the control box to the wall, the five-speed one is excellent, and send the two phase and neutral wires of the electric line to it.

From the other two terminals, clearly indicated in the instruction leaflet, start the two cables that you will send to the ceiling and which you will connect with those coming from the two terminals of the motor.

Naturally the earth cable travels on its own and is connected to a screw in contact with the metal body of the fan.

If you also intend to use the thermostat, the two wires coming from the control box must be connected to the specific thermostat terminals.

This is mounted on the ceiling, inside the upper cap.

The two cables coming from the fan motor must be connected as follows: one to the thermostat output and one directly to the neutral of the line.

As always, all these connections are made after disconnecting the voltage by acting on the main switch.

Upgrading your electrical panel

Upgrading your electrical panel is an important task that requires caution. An outdated or overloaded electrical panel can lead to electrical hazards, including fires and electrical shocks.

When upgrading your electrical panel, it's important to consider factors such as the size of your home, the electrical demands of your appliances and devices, and any future plans for home renovations.

It's important to never attempt to upgrade your electrical panel yourself, as it can be extremely dangerous and even life-threatening if not done in the proper manner.

Step-by-step electrician projects

Finally, here some step-by-step guides for your electricians repair system.

1. **Replace a light switch**

To replace a wall switch you need:

- ✓ A new switch.
- ✓ Screwdriver.

To replace an electric switch, it is then necessary to proceed by following these 9 steps:

- ✓ Cut off the power to the home system and close the circuit breaker switch.
- ✓ Remove the electrical plate.
- ✓ Extract the switch using a screwdriver.
- ✓ Disconnect the lead wires.
- ✓ Keep on taking the new switch.
- ✓ Connect the lead wires into the terminals of the new switch.
- ✓ Insert the new switch into the plastic holder.
- ✓ Complete the operation by reassembling the plate.
- ✓ To check the operation of the new switch, arm the circuit breaker and apply current.

2. **Install a ceiling fan**

To install a ceiling fan, you can look at the mini guide in the previous paragraphs.

3. **Replace a light fixture**

- ✓ Turn off the power supply: first of all, turn off the power supply of the system that powers the lighting to be replaced. This can be done by turning off the corresponding switch in the electrical control panel.
- ✓ Take away the existing lighting: unscrew the lighting fixing screws and eliminate the cover to access the electric cable. Disconnect the lighting power wires from the electrical system power supply.
- ✓ Install the new light fixture base: Make sure the new light fixture base is suitable for the bulb and wattage of your existing electrical system. Install the new base using the fixing screws provided.
- ✓ Connect the electrical wires: connect the lighting wires to the power wires of the electrical system.
- ✓ Fix the new lighting: Fix the new lighting to the base using the fixing screws provided.
- ✓ Turn on the power supply: Turn on the power supply of the electrical system and turn on the corresponding switch to turn on the light fixture. Check that the appliance is working properly.
- ✓ Check installation security: Check that the installation of the lighting is secure and that all wires are well connected and secure. Check that the new foundation is solid and stable.

4. Replace a circuit breaker

Replacing an RCD or circuit breaker requires some electrical skills and safety precautions, so it's important to be careful throughout the process to avoid injury or damage to the electrical system. Here is a general guide on how to replace a circuit breaker:

- ✓ Turn Off Electrical Power: First, turn off the electrical power to the facility that supplies power to the circuit breaker being replaced. This can be done by turning off the corresponding main switch in the electrical control panel.
- ✓ Remove the existing circuit breaker: unscrew the circuit breaker fixing screws and remove it from the electrical panel. Disconnect the circuit breaker feed wires from the electrical system feeder.
- ✓ Install the new circuit breaker: Make sure the new circuit breaker is suitable for the wattage and type of existing electrical system. Install the new circuit breaker into the electrical panel, being careful to seat it in the correct slot.
- ✓ Connect Electrical Wires: Connect circuit breaker wires to electrical system power wires.
- ✓ Fix the new circuit breaker: Fix the new circuit breaker in the panel using the fixing screws provided.
- ✓ Turn on the power supply: Turn on the power supply of the electrical system and turn on the corresponding main switch to turn on the circuit breaker. Verify that the circuit breaker is working properly.
- ✓ Verify secure installation: Check that the circuit breaker installation is secure and that all wires are properly connected and secure. Verify that the circuit breaker is securely fastened to the electrical panel.

5. Install a new smoke detector

A smoke detector gives an alarm signal once it detects smoke or gas, which can be considered as an indirectly answer to fires. For home employ smoke detectors are the most commonly utilized kinds.

Inappropriate locations for a smoke detector

There are several places where it is not appropriate to install a smoke detector due to possible frequent false alarms:

- ✓ Places where steam is present, like the shower/bathroom or kitchen.
- ✓ Near a ventilation opening, a heater or a radiator. In these locations, air convection can prevent smoke from reaching the smoke detector.
- ✓ In the garage, where exhaust fumes can cause false alarms.
- ✓ Near lamps.

A smoke detector should be installed at least 1.7 inches away from a lamp.

Smoke detector in the escape route

Smoke detectors must be installed in escape routes from the house. So, you can always be sure which way to leave the house. The right place to put a smoke detector is on the ceiling. If your home has more than one floor, placing one smoke alarm per floor may be vital. It is important that you can hear the alarm signal from the smoke detectors from the bedrooms. If you have more than one smoke detector, it is best if they are linked together.

Installation

Remove the cover and place the smoke detector on the ceiling. Mark the holes to be drilled in the ceiling. Then drill the holes to the needed depth with a 0.23 inches brick or wood drill bit and place the dowels into the holes. Then screw the smoke detector into place. The best place to mount your smoke detector is in the center of the room.

Smoke detector activation

Arrange the batteries in the battery holder and substitute the cover. Now utilize the test button to verify that the smoke detector is functional. Each smoke detector emits a warning signal to give information about low batteries need to be changed.

6. **Install a new doorbell**

- ✓ Connect the phase (brown wire) to your doorbell button. You can also connect the neutral cable if the doorbell purchased has no particular indications.
- ✓ Make a jumper, as you can see in the guide on adding an electrical outlet, between the button and your ringer. In practice you have to cut a piece of electric cable and connect the button and ringer together with a direct connection.
- ✓ The neutral cable should be linked to the free terminal of the ringtone.
- ✓ Now you can turn on the electricity again and try to ring the doorbell or through your video entry phone.

Ended the discussion about electrician homemade repairs, let's see, in the next part of the guide all you have to know about repairing and improving Heating, Ventilation, and Air Conditioning (HVAC)

PART 5: Heating, Ventilation, and Air Conditioning (HVAC)

In this chapter, readers will learn how to keep and repair their heating, ventilation, and air conditioning systems. Topics covered include replacing air filters, cleaning air ducts, and installing programmable thermostats.

Basic HVAC maintenance and repairs

Heating, ventilation and air conditioning systems are known as HVAC. Anyway, to function properly and to guarantee thermal comfort within the different structures, they are based on various kinds of equipment, applications and principles.

However, if you have this type of system here are some simple basics.

An HVAC system has some specific characteristics.

The integration of different systems makes it possible to optimize the management of internal comfort, an objective to which each individual system makes a specific contribution.

Obviously, some functions can be offered by the same system, for example by heating and cooling the environment using a single air conditioner. In fact, modern devices are increasingly advanced and capable of performing various functions, an aspect that allows for a reduction in size, facilitating control of the internal microclimate and optimizing purchase, installation and maintenance costs.

These functions can also be performed by different machines, the important thing is that they are interconnected and capable of communicating with each other to maximize comfort and minimize energy consumption and waste. In fact, a fundamental feature is also the sustainability of these systems, which must guarantee low energy consumption to offer benefits in economic and environmental terms.

Another essential aspect of an HVAC system is the high level of technology. The most advanced summer and winter ventilation and air conditioning systems are able to connect to the network, to be controlled remotely via app and integrate with home automation. Some devices allow you to monitor energy consumption and system performance, up to self-diagnosis to improve maintenance and reduce any failures and malfunctions.

Nonetheless, like any other heavy-duty equipment, HVAC units need to be well maintained to keep them in excellent operating condition. Downtime isn't just a nuisance; it can mean the building shutting down completely until the faults are fixed...and nobody wants to go that far.

How often should maintenance be scheduled? What is the maintenance that can be performed independently? Finally, what can you do to stay productive when your commonly used HVAC units are shut down for maintenance or repairs?

Maintaining your HVAC system protects your equipment and those who use it, at home or at work. So, begin with some actions you can do yourself, reducing the risk of breakdowns.

- ✓ Replace cooling equipment filters.
- ✓ Clean the air ducts every 2 years.
- ✓ Clean condenser, but also drip pan evaporator coils, blower assembly and ignition system.
- ✓ Lubricate all moving parts, including motors.
- ✓ Clean and adjust dampers annually.
- ✓ Check the coolant level and top up if necessary.
- ✓ Check the thermostat, safety controls, fan and blower motors to be sure enough they are operating properly.

With the arrival of cold weather, perform the general checks, tests and cleaning activities described above again. Furthermore:

- ✓ Replace filters on heating equipment.
- ✓ Check the heat exchanger and burner assembly.
- ✓ Carry out careful checks to locate any gas leaks.

Next phase: scheduled maintenance. Any operation more complicated than these routine tasks should definitely be left to an expert in these systems. Do-it-yourself can lead to more trouble and be expensive, while proper maintenance at reasonable intervals will prolong the life of the system.

Specific preventive maintenance needs will change based on the employ, but as a general rule thorough professional maintenance is needed before it gets too hot for your cooling system and just before it gets cold for your heating. This can be referred to a minimum of twice a year, every spring and every autumn, if your system is for cooling and heating, including boiler maintenance.

Replacing filters and thermostats

As far as the filters are concerned, specifically, before replacing them, you will have to understand if this operation actually needs to be performed. Therefore, first of all, identify the filters with the help of the instruction manual and unlock them by extracting them from the split.

To wash the filters (simple plastic grids that prevent the entry of pollen, dust, bacteria and pollutants) just use warm water with a little dishwashing liquid.

Rinse well and, before putting them back in their place, dry them with a cloth and in the air in a closed environment to avoid getting it dirty again.

As a final step, you can use disinfectant sprays to sanitize the air conditioner or sanitizing foams containing solvents and alcohol.

The cleaning of the filters, in case of intense use, should be performed once a month.

If you notice damage to the filters or if the dirt is particularly stubborn, give up: you will have to replace them. Air filters need to be replaced every four months and more frequently if you have pets in the house.

Replacing the air filter is fast and simple. This can be the tricky part, just know that there are many places it could be placed. In different systems, the filters are placed in the return air duct. This is what pulls the air back from your space into the air handler system.

The other potentially difficult part is being sure you're employing the right filters. Filter dimensions can be usually founded on the side of the filter.

Regarding the Check the correct connection and reinstall the plate in the cassette. Lastly, reapply the finishing , the necessary tools will be:

- ✓ A screwdriver kit.
- ✓ A voltage meter.
- ✓ A level.

The steps to follow instead:
- ✓ Before starting, cut off the power to the boiler.
- ✓ Remove the old thermostat.
- ✓ Remove the battery protection tab.
- ✓ Turn the lock 1/4 turn counterclockwise, using a suitable flat screwdriver, and separate the thermostat from its base.
- ✓ Open the terminal cover and lift it up until it locks.
- ✓ Fix the base with the appropriate screws and dowels or directly on the built-in support if you have one.
- ✓ Check the level before closing.
- ✓ Open the terminal cover and lift it up until it locks.
- ✓ Connect the wires on terminals 2 and 3.
- ✓ Close the terminal block cover well and screw it tightly, so as not to hinder the insertion of the mask.
- ✓ Insert the mask from above and position it, then close the safety by turning 1/4 of a turn clockwise.
- ✓ Adjust the thermostat, then connect the boiler to the power supply again, put it in heating mode and check that the thermostat is working properly.

Installing a new HVAC system: a step-by-step project

Here is a step-by-step project that you will need to install a new HVAC system. Let's begin:

Replace an air filter

We have already explained to you in the second paragraph of this guide how to replace an air filter.

Clean the air ducts

Reclaiming the air ducts is an operation that must be done periodically using specific products for sanitizing the air ducts.

Cleaning and sanitizing aeraulic channels are essential to guarantee not only the efficiency of the systems themselves, but also the quality of the air in an indoor environment and the health of the people who occupy it.

Using specific disinfectant products and substances for these operations ensures both correct cleaning and the elimination of microbiological contaminants, which can be harmful to health if inhaled. Dirt, dust, particulate matter and pathogenic microorganisms accumulate over time inside the air ducts, on the external Air Handling Unit and on the points of discontinuity of the systems (such as the heat exchange coils, the dampers, the flaps or the filters). (bacteria, molds, spores, fungi, viruses).

These components, in addition to hindering the correct and regular exchange of air, can constitute a serious source of chemical and microbiological contamination of the air.

And it is precisely unhealthy indoor air that is the main cause of Sick Building Syndrome, a pathology that involves the occupants of buildings and indoor environments equipped with degraded and inefficient mechanical ventilation or air conditioning systems.

Proper ordinary and extraordinary maintenance of the aeraulic systems is essential for:
- ✓ Increase the efficiency of the system itself, reducing energy costs.
- ✓ Make indoor air better and breathable.
- ✓ Eliminate any possible dust and pollen allergens.
- ✓ Reduce the concentration of bacteria, viruses, molds and fungi that may be present.
- ✓ Check for the presence of bacterium and then proceed with their elimination.

Cleaning, disinfection, sanitization. Three different terms, but which we often tend to confuse by mistakenly using them as synonyms. When talking about such an important topic as the maintenance of air ducts, however, it is advisable to clarify:

1. Cleaning is a set of manual and/or mechanical operations aimed at removing visible dirt from an environment or surface.

2. Sanitization is an intervention aimed at eradicating bacteria and contaminants that normal cleaning activities cannot remove.
3. Disinfection consists in the use of chemical or physical disinfectant agents (for example heat) capable of destroying or inactivating the pathogenic microorganisms present on the surfaces to be treated.

Cleaning is an essential preliminary operation for the purposes of the subsequent sanitization and disinfection phases. Therefore, there will be no sanitization and disinfection if the dirt is not first removed with water and/or specific detergents.

The removal of dirt is essential for the success of the subsequent disinfection and sanitization phases, which is carried out using particular chemical detergent products which bring the microbial load inside the ducts back to acceptable hygiene standards.

As far as actual cleaning is concerned, the air ducts are usually cleaned using any mechanical means that allows the removal of dust and dirt.

There are different systems for cleaning the air ducts, but among the most used there are:
1. Blowing.
2. Brushing.
3. Compressed air.

All three systems must then be integrated with the use of an aspirator, necessary to convey the removed dirt outside.

The most used is certainly brushing: but how does it happen?

Brushing basically consists in the use of a rotating brush which is introduced inside the air duct. Once the external electric motor has been activated, the brush will begin to raise dust and dirt which will then be removed by means of a vacuum cleaner.

But how exactly does this procedure work?
- ✓ The channel is divided into sections ranging from 50 meters to 100 meters.
- ✓ The air vents are suitably sealed and isolated to prevent contaminants from escaping and dispersing in the internal environment.
- ✓ A maximum depression is created in the center of the segment to be reclaimed, and close to zero on the walls of the same, by applying an aspirator.
- ✓ The mechanical brushes, rotating clockwise and counterclockwise, remove the solid residues and simultaneously with the suction, lift them up to the maximum suction point.
- ✓ Dust and dirt deposits are captured and conveyed inside the fan of the vacuum cleaner equipped with absolute filters.

Install a programmable thermostat

A programmable thermostat gives you more control options and saves you money on heating and cooling your home. It allows you to set different temperatures for different times of day and even for different times on different days. In cold months, you can set it to automatically lower the temperature when you leave for work and raise it an hour before you get home. You can do the same when it comes to cooling during the hot months. This way your furnace or air conditioner doesn't run all day and wastes fuel or electricity when the house is unoccupied.

Choose a thermostat that gives accurate readings, usually within about one degree of the set temperatures. Thermostats that allow for two-to-three-degree swings in temperature significantly reduce the efficiency and comfort of your home.

Step 1: Unplug and remove the old thermostat.

Shut off the power to the furnace or air conditioner. Even if the thermostat wires are low voltage, the oven electronics can be damaged by a short if you touch live wires during installation.

Unplug the wires from the old thermostat. Now you have 4 wires to disconnect. Keep the disconnected wires from sliding back into the wall by temporarily wrapping them around a pencil.

Step 2: Install the new thermostat.

Every thermostat terminal can be identified through a letter, and each of the wires is different color identification. Note which string goes to each letter and write the letter on a small piece of tape attached to each string. The wire colors may not connect to the same terminals as the new thermostat - always follow the letter code.

Fit the new wall plate. If the screw holes do not line up with the existing mounting plate holes, mark the new locations and drill the holes, then install wall anchors if needed for the new mounting plate.

Attach the wires to the terminal screws, matching the letters on the wires to the letters on the new drive.

Install the batteries into the thermostat and snap the cover into place.

Step 3: Program the thermostat

Check and apply the manufacturer's instructions for setting the new thermostat. The basic temperature settings are the same, but the new unit will allow you to set multiple times to turn heating or cooling on and off. For example, you can set up a work week schedule and a weekend schedule, as well as a nightly setback schedule.

Install a new air conditioner

Here's how to install an air conditioner in 7 steps:

1. Choose the type of air conditioner

If you are looking for instructions on how to assemble an air conditioner yourself, you should have clear in mind which model you are interested in. You may find several types of air conditioners.

To choose the right one for your home, you need to evaluate the size, number of rooms to refresh, budget available.

Here are the most popular air conditioner models on the market.

1. Air conditioner without outdoor unit: undemanding and bulky, ideal for refrigerating a room.
2. Air conditioner with outdoor unit: essential if you want to install the air conditioning system in several rooms or in just one, with the guarantee of high performance.
3. Monosplit air conditioner: it has an external unit (motor) and an internal one.
4. Multisplit air conditioner: it has an outdoor unit and several indoor units; among the most used is the dual split, which connects two air conditioners to one engine.
5. Air conditioner with inverter technology allows you to regulate the operation of the system according to the external and internal climatic conditions, and therefore allows you to optimize resources and consumption.
6. Air conditioner with ducted system: ducting allows fresh air to be circulated in every part of a large house, without installing numerous indoor units.

2. Choose where to mount the air conditioner

The question to ask yourself is not only how an air conditioner is mounted, but also where it is best to install it.

When you buy the air conditioner, you will find instructions for choosing the location and correct assembly of the device in the instruction booklet.

In any case, it may be useful to know in advance the general rules on identifying where to mount the air conditioner and how.

For the indoor unit:

✓ Place the air conditioning system at a minimum height of 6.56 feet from the floor: this prevents dust from entering and the formation of condensation on the ceiling.

✓ Make sure there are no obstacles within a radius of 15 or 30 cm to facilitate the correct flow of air.

✓ The chosen location must be easily accessible for future maintenance.

For the outdoor unit:

✓ Choose a terrace, courtyard or garden that is easily accessible.

✓ Find the best location to contain the visual and acoustic impact.

✓ Create a support or pedestal about 5.9 inches from the floor on which to place the outdoor unit: this will prevent contact with water, leaves and dirt.

✓ Be certain of the fact that your device is protected from the elements as much as possible.

4. Mount the outdoor unit.

You must have a great knowledge of systems to know how to assemble an air conditioner in all its parts, internal and external.

If you have chosen a mono-split or multi-split air conditioner with an outdoor unit, the installation work is certainly challenging.

The external compressor is bulky and heavy: it can reach a weight of a few tens of kilos. To secure it, you need to create brackets for the outdoor unit to rest on.

It uses solid materials and insulating protectors to cushion the machine's shocks and vibrations during operation.

4. Prepare the drain piping.

Each air conditioning system has its own condensate drain system, i.e. drops of water.

If you want to learn how to install an air conditioner yourself in an exemplary way, you need to locate a drain near the area where you intend to install the air conditioner.

The best thing you can do is evaluate this need before you even get started, i.e. when you're in the design phase of the job.

Therefore, having a nearby drain available, it is necessary to prepare the corrugated or PVC pipes that connect the air conditioner to the drain, in order to dispose of the condensate.

If it is not possible to make the drainpipes, collect the condensate in a container which you will have to empty periodically.

5. Set the electrical connections.

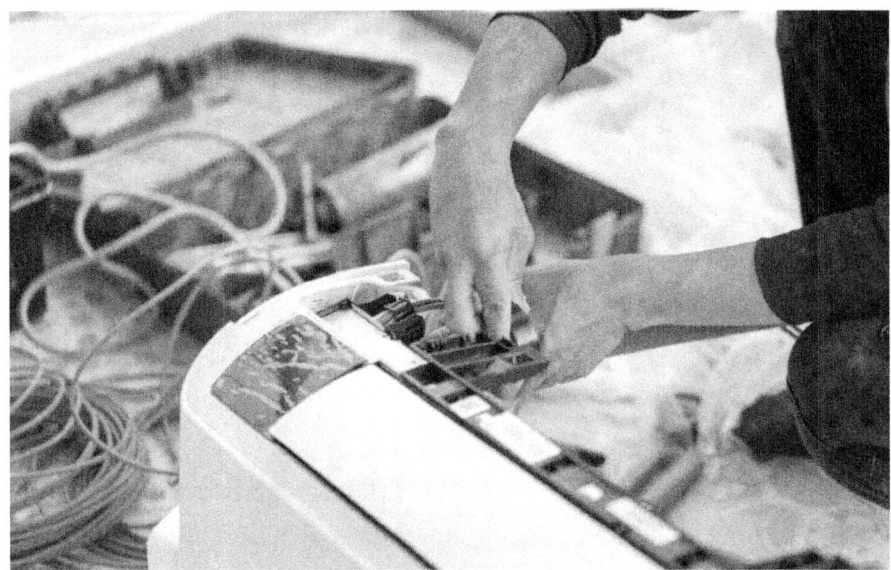

Make sure that all parts of the air conditioning system can be easily connected to the electrical system.

Bring the electricity cables to where they are needed and prepare the connections.

This could be a very complicated job for someone who is not an expert in plants. The ideal would be to drill the wall and insert a 2.36 inches diameter pipe. This pipe should be installed on an incline, guaranteeing a slope of 15%.

The pipe created, preferably in PVC, is perfect for passing both the condensate drain pipe and the electric cable.

6. Install the air conditioner.

There is a secret on how to mount an air conditioner and make it anchored to the wall in a firm and stable way.

First, a metal support called a template must be mounted on the wall.

Once this support is installed, you can move on to mounting the air conditioner by following these step-by-step operations.

- ✓ Connect all pipes to the air conditioning machine.
- ✓ Use the hardware kit that came with your air conditioner to install, secure, and tighten all fittings.
- ✓ If you use an outdoor unit, go outside and repeat the step: connect cables and pipes to the outdoor unit.
- ✓ Place the air conditioner on the wall in the exact position where you want to mount it; fix it to the template and for greater security seal the edges with silicone or sealing foam.
- ✓ Install any external casing of the air conditioner.
- ✓ Make the necessary touch-ups on the walls: fix the whitewashing and remedy any cracks, holes or burrs created during the work in progress.
- ✓ Connect the appliance to the electrical socket and put it into operation.

7. Run a function test.

When you turn on the air conditioner for the first time, carefully observe its operation and carry out a thorough check.

Pay attention to these factors:
- ✓ The connecting pipes must not leak.
- ✓ Correct presence of the refrigeration gas.
- ✓ Correct presence of water.
- ✓ Perfect assembly of each component of the indoor unit and of the outdoor unit.
- ✓ Vibrations or noises produced by the air conditioner or external compressor.
- ✓ Pay close attention and try to understand every slightest anomaly.

Install a humidifier or dehumidifier

To install a humidifier or a dehumidifier in your home, follow these general steps:

Installing a Humidifier

Choose the right type of humidifier: There are different types of humidifiers available, such as central humidifiers that connect to your HVAC system, evaporative humidifiers, or ultrasonic humidifiers. Select the one that best suits your needs and budget.

Select the location: Determine the area in your home where you want to install the humidifier. Common locations include the central HVAC system or specific rooms.

Prepare the installation area: Clear the installation area and ensure there is proper space and access to water and power sources.

Check and apply the manufacturer's instructions: so, check properly the instruction manual provided by the manufacturer for specific installation guidelines. This may include mounting the humidifier unit, connecting it to the water supply, and wiring it to a power source.

Connect the water supply: Depending on the type of humidifier, you may need to connect it to a water source. This could involve tapping into a water line or using a reservoir that needs to be manually filled.

Connect the power supply: Ensure the power to the unit is turned off before making any electrical connections. Follow the manufacturer's instructions for wiring the humidifier to a power source, such as an electrical outlet or the HVAC system.

Test and adjust: Once the humidifier is installed, turn on the power and test the unit to ensure it is working properly. Adjust the humidity settings as desired and monitor the humidity levels in your home to maintain a comfortable and healthy environment.

Installing a Dehumidifier

Choose the appropriate dehumidifier: Select a dehumidifier based on the size and moisture level of the area you want to dehumidify. Options include portable dehumidifiers or whole-house dehumidifiers that can be integrated into your HVAC system.

Determine the location: Identify the area where you want to install the dehumidifier. Basements, crawl spaces, or rooms with high humidity levels are common locations.

Prepare the installation area: Clear the installation area and ensure there is adequate space for the dehumidifier. Make sure there is a nearby power source and proper drainage options for the condensate water.

Check the instruction manual given with the manufacturer for specific installation instructions. This may involve mounting the dehumidifier, connecting it to a power source, and setting up drainage.

Connect to power: Ensure the power is turned off before making any electrical connections. Connect the dehumidifier to a nearby electrical outlet or follow the manufacturer's instructions for wiring it into the electrical system.

Set up drainage: Dehumidifiers remove moisture from the air, and the water collected needs to be drained. Follow the manufacturer's instructions to set up proper drainage, which could involve connecting a hose to a floor drain or using a condensate pump.

Test and adjust: Once the dehumidifier is installed, turn on the power and test the unit to ensure it is functioning correctly. Adjust the settings based on the desired humidity level and monitor the moisture levels in your home.

Install a ductless mini-split system

Installing a ductless mini-split system can be a great solution for heating and cooling specific areas or rooms in a home without the need for extensive ductwork. Below we will give you a general overview of the installation process:

- ✓ Assess your needs: Determine the areas or rooms where you want to install the ductless mini-split system. Consider factors such as the size of the space, insulation, and heat load requirements.
- ✓ Select the right system: Choose a ductless mini-split system that is appropriate for your needs in terms of cooling and heating capacity. Consider energy efficiency ratings, features, and the reputation of the manufacturer.
- ✓ Choose indoor and outdoor units. The indoor unit is mounted inside the room, while the outdoor unit is put outside the house. Select the appropriate size and style of indoor unit based on the aesthetics and functional requirements of the space.
- ✓ Determine the installation location: Decide where to mount the indoor and outdoor units. The indoor unit is typically placed high on a wall or sometimes on the ceiling. The outdoor unit is usually placed on a stable surface outside the building, such as a concrete pad or mounting brackets.
- ✓ Install refrigerant lines and electrical connections: Connect the indoor and outdoor units employing some refrigerant lines. Electrical wiring must also be installed to power the system. This step requires knowledge of electrical work and refrigeration systems, so it is recommended to hire a professional HVAC technician.
- ✓ Install condensate drainage: A condensate drainage line needs to be installed to carry away the moisture produced by the cooling process. It should be properly routed to a suitable drainage point, such as a floor drain or external outlet.
- ✓ Test and commission the system: Once the installation is complete, the system should be thoroughly tested to ensure proper operation. The HVAC technician will check refrigerant levels, airflow, and temperature differentials to verify that the system is working correctly.

Add a smart thermostat and control system

To add a smart thermostat and control system to your HVAC setup, follow these general steps:
- ✓ **Choose a compatible smart thermostat**: Research and select a smart thermostat that is compatible with your existing HVAC system. Consider factors such as compatibility with your heating and cooling equipment, connectivity options, features, and compatibility with smart home ecosystems like Google Home or Amazon Alexa.
- ✓ **Turn off power:** Before starting any installation work, turn off the power to your HVAC system at the breaker box to ensure safety.
- ✓ **Take away the old thermostat:** eliminate the cover of your existing thermostat and disconnect the wiring from the terminals. Take note of the wire labels to ensure proper connection with the new thermostat.
- ✓ **Install the smart thermostat base:** Mount the smart thermostat base onto the wall using the provided screws and anchors. Ensure that the base is level.

- ✓ **Connect the wiring:** Connect the wiring from your HVAC system to the corresponding terminals on the smart thermostat base. Follow the manufacturer's instructions or refer to the wiring labels from the previous thermostat. Double-check the connections to ensure accuracy.
- ✓ **Attach the smart thermostat:** Attach the smart thermostat to the base by aligning it properly and gently snapping it into place. Make sure it is securely attached.
- ✓ **Power on and configure the smart thermostat**: Turn on the power to your HVAC system at the breaker box. The smart thermostat should power up. Follow the manufacturer's instructions to configure the thermostat settings, including connecting it to your home's Wi-Fi network and setting up any desired scheduling or automation features.
- ✓ **Install the corresponding smartphone app:** Download and install the smartphone app provided by the smart thermostat manufacturer. This app will allow you to control and monitor your HVAC system remotely.
- ✓ **Set up smart home integration:** If desired, you can integrate your smart thermostat with your smart home ecosystem. Follow the instructions provided by the smart thermostat manufacturer or the smart home platform you are using (e.g., Google Home, Amazon Alexa) to link and control your thermostat through voice commands or automation routines.
- ✓ **Test and fine-tune:** Once the installation and setup are complete, test the smart thermostat to ensure it is functioning properly. Verify that you can adjust the temperature, create schedules, and remotely control the thermostat through the smartphone app or smart home integration.

Upgrading your insulation and weatherization

Upgrading insulation and weatherization are both effective measures for improving the energy efficiency of a building and reducing heat loss or heat gain. Those are:

Insulation

Insulation can be a true aid for minimizing heat transfer between the interior and exterior of a building. It is typically installed in the walls, roof, floors, and other areas where heat loss or gain can occur. By adding insulation, you can create a thermal barrier that reduces the need for heating or cooling, resulting in energy savings and improved comfort. There are some kinds of insulation materials available, such as fiberglass, cellulose, spray foam, and rigid foam boards, each with its own advantages and applications.

Weatherization

Weatherization involves sealing and insulating a building to prevent air leakage and drafts. This process typically includes sealing gaps and cracks around windows, doors, vents, and other openings to minimize air infiltration. Weatherization can be an improving of the efficiency of heating, ventilation, and air conditioning (HVAC) systems and optimizing their performance. By reducing unwanted air exchange, weatherization helps maintain a more stable indoor temperature and reduces the energy required for heating or cooling.

Combining insulation and weatherization can have significant energy-saving benefits. Insulation primarily addresses heat transfer through conduction and convection, while weatherization focuses on reducing air leakage and drafts, which can also contribute to heat loss and gain.

When considering upgrading insulation and weatherization in a building, it's advisable to conduct an energy audit or consult with professionals who specialize in energy efficiency. They can assess the current insulation levels, identify areas of air leakage, and recommend appropriate insulation materials and weatherization strategies tailored to your specific building and climate conditions.

Remember that local building codes and regulations should be followed when undertaking insulation or weatherization projects to ensure compliance and safety.

The fifth chapter has also come to an end. In the next we will shift our attention to Carpentry and Woodworking.

PART 6: Carpentry and Woodworking

This chapter covers basic carpentry and woodworking tasks such as installing baseboards and building simple furniture pieces. More advanced tasks like installing barn doors and building custom bookshelves are also covered.

Basic carpentry skills

When we talk about carpentry we mean the preparation of reinforcements, formwork, support structures in wood and iron, before moving on to concrete castings, the raising of brick, cellular concrete or plasterboard walls. The carpentry tools that are needed in this phase are not many and can already be part of the standard equipment. speaking of DIY carpentry basics, here's what you'll need to have in your home, for your repairs or improvements:

✓ **The nail bag,** which is secured to the waist, allows us to have the nails for making formwork, measuring instruments, hammers and other tools close at hand.

- ✓ A hoist is essential to lift weights on scaffolding. There are light versions, which can be mounted on a mobile arm.
- ✓ **Angle grinder:** used to cut and shape the iron of the armor, but also to engrave concrete, stone, bricks, and various metals. Different types of discs are used for these jobs.

- ✓ **Long spikes:** long spikes are needed to pass through the beams with the largest section and to be able to fasten the structures. In most cases the attack is of the SDS type.

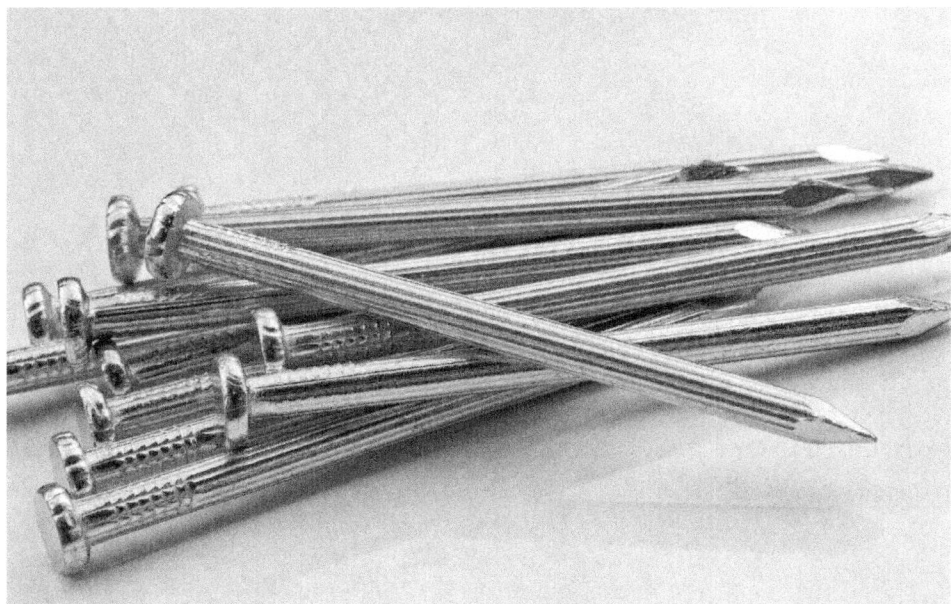

- ✓ **Screwdriver drill:** indispensable in many situations and needs in the assembly of wooden structures. The battery-powered version equipped with angular transmission is particularly practical.

✓ **Chain saw:** its great cutting capacity allows you to remove the end parts of wooden beams, shape panels and more, especially in the construction of roof support structures.

✓ **Manual saw:** used to cut smaller section elements during the construction of formwork, roofs, sheds. The electric reciprocating saw can fully replace it and also cuts metal.

- **Claw hammer:** equipped with a beating head and a nail remover pen, it has a fairly long handle and is provided, on the head, with two recesses in which to house the nail and drive it in with one hand.

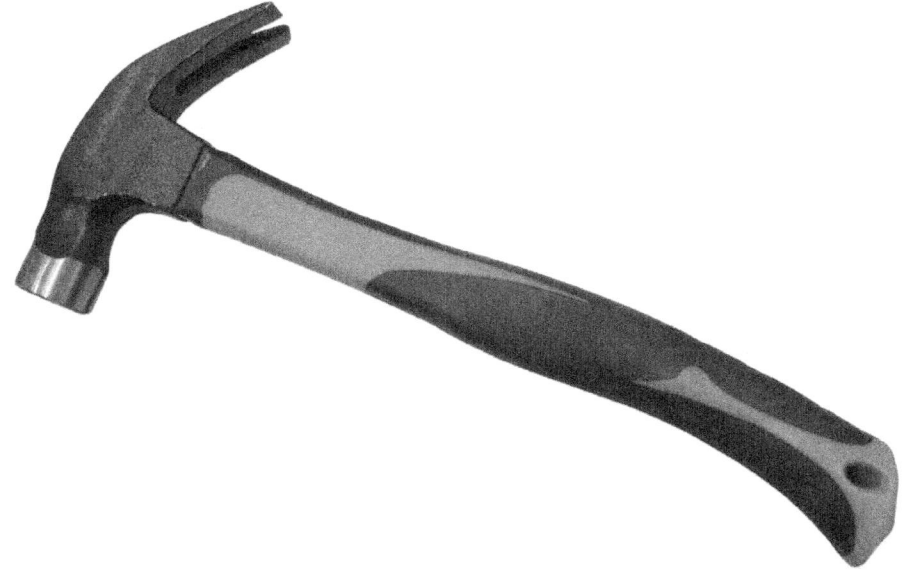

Here are 3 useful tips for your basic carpentry business:

Invest in tools and equipment

Buying tools like the ones just mentioned and quality equipment is a truly important step in applying carpentry. Woodworking tools are almost all available at most hardware stores.

These tools are expensive, but so high in performance and results.

Set a dedicated workspace

Setting a dedicated workspace is vital when it comes to do carpentry. Carpentry requires concentration and careful planning. You also need to consider the space you intend to occupy when working on projects.

A proper workspace can give us the necessary tools and materials, making it easier to organize and access all the required equipment. Also, it offers a safe and clean environment. You never want your children or family members to get into an accident.

Repairing or replacing damaged trim and molding

Replacing damaged trim and molding can help restore the aesthetics of your home. Here are the general steps to follow:

- ✓ **Gather the necessary tools and materials:** You will typically need a pry bar, a hammer, a utility knife, a tape measure, a miter saw or a coping saw, nails or screws, a caulk gun, and paint or stain for finishing.
- ✓ **Remove the damaged trim:** Use the pry bar and hammer to carefully remove the damaged trim. Start at one end and gently pry it away from the wall or surface. Be cautious not to damage the surrounding area.
- ✓ **Take measurements and purchase replacement trim:** employ a tape measure to determine the length and width of the trim that needs to be replaced. Take note of any special angles or corners that may require mitering or coping. Purchase the appropriate replacement trim from a hardware store.
- ✓ **Cut the replacement trim:** Use a miter saw or coping saw to cut the replacement trim to the correct length and angles. Take care to make precise cuts, especially for corners and joints.
- ✓ **Install the new trim:** Place the replacement trim in position and secure it with nails or screws. Employ a nail punch to set the nails under the surface. Ensure the trim is level and flush with the surrounding surfaces.
- ✓ **Fill gaps and holes:** Use a caulk gun to apply caulk or wood filler to any gaps or nail holes in the trim.
- ✓ **Sand and finish:** Once the caulk or filler is dry, sand the patched areas to create a smooth surface. If necessary, apply paint or stain to match the color of the existing trim. Let the paint or stain to a total dry.

Remember to work carefully and patiently when replacing trim and molding to achieve a professional-looking result.

Building custom shelves and cabinets

Making your own furniture requires some preparation. Some tools are required. It is useful to make a working drawing in advance and think well in advance of all the parts of your custom-made furniture.

What are the elements needed to make a piece of furniture?

Different materials are needed to make a piece of furniture. The exact requirement depends on the project. This list gives you an overview of the materials you may need:

- Graph paper, pencil, eraser, ruler: for furniture design.
- Cordless drill: for easy pre-drilling of holes and driving screws into the material (tip: also use a depth stop or dowel drill set to limit the drilling depth).
- Wood glue and glue tongs: can be used as needed to glue several boards together.
- Dowels, corner joints or slats - depending on how you want to connect the different furniture parts.
- Lamello cutter.
- Dowels, corner joints or slats - depending on how you want to connect the different furniture parts.
- Sandpaper - always useful to have on hand, to smooth out irregularities or smooth out holes.
- Tape measure or folding rule: to take the exact measurements of the piece of furniture and order the material in sheets of the right size.
- Screws: to connect the various parts together
- Putty: Can be used to neatly cover the screw holes
- Spirit level: to build everything perfectly straight.

How do you make a drawing or sketch of a custom cut piece of furniture?

Before starting work on your custom furniture, it is good to think carefully about the design. How many shelves will the cabinet have? Will it have doors or drawers? Will it need a back panel? You also need to know the exact dimensions of all panel materials.

So, make a good drawing or sketch of your furniture. You can do this with a digital program, like SketchUp or Free CAD. But even a sketch with pencil, graph paper, ruler and eraser is fine.

While sketching, also think about how to connect the different slab materials. Will you be using corner anchors, dowels or slats?

We can also cut the panel material obliquely. This creates invisible joints. For more information, see our finish options.

To see how the piece of furniture will fit into the room, tape the outside measurements of the piece of furniture to the wall with masking tape. This will give you a good idea of the dimensions of the furniture and allow you to modify the design if necessary.

Ultimately, it's all about drawing up the sketch so you know the exact measurements of all the materials you need. When doing so, also take into account the external and internal dimensions.

Are you building a built-in wardrobe or wardrobe? Then remember that no house is completely straight. Measure at multiple points, such as between the ceiling and the floor. This is essential for a built-in wardrobe, to avoid any unpleasant surprises later.

What are the components of a made-to-measure piece of furniture?

When building a piece of furniture, you usually aren't limited to sheet material. You may have equipped your project with doors, drawers and other elements that many wardrobes cannot do without.

Doors and drawers.

When installing doors and drawers, it is important to pay close attention to the quality of the hinges and drawer slides. Look for the right hinges or drawer slides for your project.

If your project includes drawers, the guides you will use must be suitable for the internal dimensions of the drawer. Inquire well in advance.

Furniture accessories.

The hardware chosen can be decisive for the final appearance of the piece of furniture. Consider the hardware you need and its role in the design.

Adjustable feet.

If the floor in your home isn't completely straight, you can put the furniture on leveling feet. This way, you can still easily level the furniture.

Back panel.

Do you want to insert a board in your furniture? Then choose a thin material, such as hardboard. You fix it, for example, with small screws.

Shelves.

Shelves are present in most wardrobes. To fix them, you must first determine the location of the holes for fixing the shelf supports. Make sure you don't drill into the shelf by screwing a fastener onto the drill bit. If you don't have a depth stop, you can also employ a piece of tape to cover the drill bit.

How do you fix a piece of furniture to the wall?

If you are making a tall piece of furniture, it is a good idea to anchor it to the wall. This will prevent the furniture from falling over. This is certainly advisable if there are small children in the house who could try to climb on the piece of furniture.

You can easily anchor the furniture to the wall by fixing it with a screw. Be quite sure you are employing a suitable dowel and, if necessary, insert a large washer under the screw head so that it does not drive through the wood.

Impact bolts or wedge bolts can also be used for anchoring. Remember that it is better to anchor a large piece of furniture in several places.

How do the sheet materials connect in the cabinet?

It is possible to connect the different shelves and slabs of the custom-made furniture in various ways.

The most obvious way is to fix the different materials with screws. However, it is good to finish the screw holes with putty. If desired, the screw connections can be reinforced by one of the methods given below.

Corner joints.

This is the simplest, but perhaps also the least beautiful way of assembling the piece of furniture. With corner joints, the different shelves are screwed tightly together.

Dowels.

Using the dowels, you can glue the different parts of the furniture tightly together. Make sure you have good equipment, such as a set of dowel drills, and mark the holes carefully. Connect the dowels to the boards with a little wood glue.

Slats.

By using the slats, you get a larger gluing surface and thus a slightly firmer joint than with dowels. For this you need a special milling machine. Our handyman Roelof used Lamello for his bedroom wardrobe.

What material do you use for a custom cut piece of furniture?

Below, we illustrate some of the materials commonly used by our craftsmen to make wardrobes.

Plywood.

Plywood panels are versatile and durable. Ideal for making wardrobes and available in different variants. Plywood looks also more natural. The most commonly used variant is birch plywood. But you can also choose a top fix layer type.

Wooden board.

Wooden planks are ideal for making your own furniture. Joinery panels are furniture panels made from solid wood. This makes them robust and of high quality. Among our craftsmen, we see a lot of use of oak, spruce and pine panels. All joinery panels have a natural look.

Installing hardwood floors or laminate flooring

Both hardwood floors and laminate flooring are popular choices for homeowners.
Installing hardwood floors and laminate flooring requires careful planning and attention to detail. Here's a general guide on how to install each type of flooring:

Installing Hardwood Floors

Prepare the Subfloor:

All you have to do is to be sure that the subfloor is clean, dry, and level. Remove any existing flooring, carpet, or debris.
Repair any cracks or uneven areas in the subfloor.

Acclimate the Hardwood:

Unwrap the hardwood flooring and let it acclimate to the room for at least 48 hours. This permits to the wood of adapting to the humidity and temperature of the space.

Install Underlayment (Optional):

Some hardwood floors require an underlayment for moisture protection or sound insulation. Check and apply the manufacturer's instructions to install it if needed.

Start Installation:

Begin installation along the longest exterior wall of the room.

Place spacers against the wall to create an expansion gap (usually around 1/2 inch) to allow for natural expansion and contraction of the wood.

Lay the first row of boards, ensuring the grooved side faces the wall.

Employ a nail gun or a pneumatic stapler to make sure the boards to the subfloor.

Continue Installation:

Install subsequent rows by fitting the tongue of each board inside the groove of the previous row.

Stagger the end joints between adjacent rows to create a more stable and aesthetically pleasing pattern.

Use a mallet and a tapping block to ensure tight and seamless connections between boards.

Trim and Finishing:

Measure and cut boards to fit around obstacles like doorways or vents using a saw.

Install baseboards or molding to cover the expansion gap around the perimeter of the room.

Installing Laminate Flooring

Set the Subfloor:

Be quite sure that the subfloor is clean, dry, and level. Remove any existing flooring, carpet, or debris.

Repair any cracks or uneven areas in the subfloor.

Acclimate the Laminate:

Unbox the laminate flooring and let it acclimate in the room for at least 48 hours.

Install Underlayment:

Laminate flooring typically needs of an underlayment to create sound insulation, cushioning, and moisture protection. Apply, after having read the manufacturer's instructions to create the underlayment.

Start Installation:

Begin installation along the longest exterior wall of the room.

Use spacers to create an expansion gap (usually around 1/4 inch) along the walls.

Lay the first row of planks with the groove side facing the wall.

Connect the planks by angling the tongue into the groove and pressing them together. Employ a tapping block and a hammer to have a certain snug fit.

Continue Installation:

Install subsequent rows by connecting the short end of one plank to another at an angle, then lowering it to lock into place.

Stagger the end joints between adjacent rows to create a more stable and visually appealing pattern.

Use a pull bar and hammer to tighten connections and ensure a flush surface.

Trim and Finishing:

Trim the last row of planks to fit against the wall, leaving an expansion gap.

Install baseboards or molding to cover the expansion gap around the perimeter of the room.

Remember, these are general instructions, and it's essential to consult the specific installation guidelines provided by the manufacturer of the hardwood or laminate flooring you're using. Additionally, consider hiring a professional installer if you're unsure or if the job requires more advanced skills.

step-by-step projects

Here some full carpentry step by step projects.

1. Build a custom bookshelf

Making customized furniture directly with your own hands means obtaining great satisfaction.

In the case of the bookcase, we are talking about a simple construction, which only provides for an external frame made up of planks of various materials and central shelving, to be modulated according to one's needs and personal taste.

Here's how:

Find the tools.

First of all, it is advisable to have all the kit necessary to complete the job at hand.

You will have to use a screwdriver drill, a set of screws of various sizes, a level to check the assembly, a meter, a square with a pencil to evaluate measurements and reference points, sandpaper, colored paint if necessary, a polish and a set of brushes.

Depending on the type of material chosen, all or only some may be needed, as in the case of raw wood that does not need to be sanded or painted.

Select items.

The bookcase is made up of a series of planks that are linked together to create the perimeter and internal structure.

If you go to a specialized shop, you can ask that the parts be shaped directly on site, while if you have chosen a recycled material you will have to proceed independently with a hacksaw and a circular saw in case of greater thickness.

The aim is to prepare each component and proceed to its treatment first.

Work the planks.

The next step is to sand each element to make it smooth and ready to use. You can use sandpaper and only then proceed with the paint, making one or more passes depending on the degree of coverage you wish to obtain.

Don't forget a polishing product that can also preserve everything from the inevitable wear and tear of time.

Create the structure.

Drill to assemble the whole library.

At this point it is necessary to lay the foundations for the external part, which will then have to support the shelves you want to insert. Employ bold screws to join the elements together and for making you pretty sure that all is solid and stable.

Decide in advance whether you will place the bookcase vertically or horizontally, so that you can work it correctly.

Fix everything with a screwdriver and only then start arranging the shelves. You can choose to follow a random order and create gradients that give dynamism or create a more classic and linear composition respecting the traditional heights and geometries.

The beauty of do-it-yourself is that you have the possibility to make changes at any time, evaluating step by step whether the initial project proves to be valid during construction. Stand the structure upright and check if it is straight and above all firm, tightening the screws where necessary and making the final touches.

Decorate

Finally, proceed with all the decorations that best represent you, so as to create a bookcase that fits perfectly with your personality and the context in which you want to place it. Beautify the bookcase by giving vent to your imagination, to create a unique piece created entirely by you!

2. **Build a window seat or bench**

To build a simple wooden window seat or bench, you'll need the following materials and tools:

Materials:
- 2x4 lumber or plywood for framing
- 1x4 lumber for the seat and backrest
- Wood screws
- Wood glue
- Sandpaper
- Primer and paint or stain
- Cushion or foam padding (optional)

Tools:
- Tape measure
- Circular saw or hand saw

- ✓ Drill
- ✓ Screwdriver
- ✓ Clamps
- ✓ Sanding block or electric sander
- ✓ Paintbrush or foam roller

Here's a step-by-step guide on how to build a window seat or bench:

Measure the space: Determine the dimensions of the window seat, considering the available space and your desired size.

Cut the frame pieces: Using the 2x4 lumber or plywood, cut four pieces for the vertical supports (two for each side) and four pieces for the horizontal supports (two for the front and two for the back). Split them to match the wish height and width of your seat.

Assemble the frame: Position the vertical supports on each side and attach the horizontal supports using wood screws and wood glue. Ensure the corners are square and the frame is sturdy. You can utilize clamps to hold the pieces together while attaching them.

Cut the seat and backrest pieces: Measure and cut the 1x4 lumber to the desired length for the seat and backrest. Cut the seat pieces to match the width of the frame and cut the backrest pieces to match the height.

Attach the seat and backrest: Place the seat pieces on top of the frame and secure them using wood screws. For more stability, you can glue the seat pieces to the frame as well. Attach the backrest pieces vertically along the back of the frame using screws and glue.

Sand and finish: Use sandpaper or an electric sander to smooth any rough edges or surfaces. Apply a primer coat and let it dry, then paint or stain the window seat according to your preference. Allow sufficient drying time between coats.

Optional: Add a cushion or foam padding: If desired, you can attach a cushion or foam padding to the seat for added comfort. Measure the dimensions of the seat and have a cushion or foam cut to fit. Attach it using fabric glue or secure it with fabric ties.

Once the paint or stain is fully dried, your window seat or bench is ready to be placed beneath the window.

Build a floating shelf

Building a floating represents a big way to bring more storage and display space to your home. Here's a general guide on how to build a simple floating shelf:

Materials you will need:

- ✓ Wood board: Choose a board that suits your desired shelf size and matches your home's aesthetic. Common options include solid wood or plywood.
- ✓ Wall brackets: Look for sturdy, concealed brackets specifically designed for floating shelves.
- ✓ Screws: Select screws appropriate for the type and thickness of your wall.

- ✓ Wall anchors (if necessary): If you're not able to screw directly into studs, wall anchors can provide additional support.
- ✓ Level
- ✓ Drill
- ✓ Screwdriver or drill bit
- ✓ Measuring tape
- ✓ Pencil
- ✓ Sandpaper
- ✓ Stain, paint, or finish (optional)

Step-by-step instructions:

Measure and mark the desired location of your shelf on the wall. Employ a stud finder to find the wall studs, as they provide the best support. If studs aren't available or not in the right position, you'll need to use wall anchors for extra stability.

Mark the locations of the brackets on the wall. Be certain that they are level and evenly spaced. Typically, two brackets are used for shorter shelves, and three or more for longer shelves.

Pre-drill holes into the wall at the marked positions. Employ an appropriate drill bit size for your screws and drill the holes directly into the wall studs.

Attach the brackets to the wall employing some screws. Be certain, at this point, that they are securely fastened.

Measure and mark the corresponding positions of the brackets on the underside of the wood board. Ensure they align with the wall brackets.

Use a screwdriver or drill to tighten the screws securely but be careful not to over-tighten and damage the wood.

Check that the shelf is level. If adjustments are needed, slightly loosen the screws and make the necessary changes.

Apply your preferred finish to the wood, such as stain, paint, or sealant, following the manufacturer's instructions. Let it dry completely.

When it's done, your floating shelf is ready to be employed!

Remember to always consider safety when working with tools and mounting items to walls.

3. **Build a wooden headboard**

Building a wooden headboard can be a fun and rewarding DIY project. Here's a step-by-step guide to help you get started. Materials you'll need:

- ✓ Wood boards (1x6 or 1x8 pine boards are commonly used)
- ✓ Measuring tape Pencil Saw (circular saw or miter saw)
- ✓ Sandpaper (medium and fine grit)
- ✓ Wood stain or paint (optional)
- ✓ Paintbrush or foam applicator (if staining or painting)

- ✓ Screws or nails
- ✓ Screwdriver or hammer Wall mounting hardware (if necessary)

Step 1: Measure and plan Measure the width of your mattress and determine the desired height of your headboard. Sketch out your design on paper, noting the dimensions and any additional features like curves or decorative cutouts.

Step 2: Gather and prepare the wood Purchase the required amount of wood boards based on your measurements. If needed, have them cut to the desired length at the store or cut them yourself using a saw.

Step 3: Put together the headboard Lay out the boards on a flat surface in the wanted arrangement. Employ some screws or nails to put the boards together, putting them at regular intervals along the seams. Make sure the boards are aligned properly as you secure them together.

Step 4: Finishing touches Sand the entire headboard to create a smooth surface. Begin with medium-grit sandpaper and complete with fine-grit sandpaper. Put it to dry completely.

Step 5: Mount the headboard Determine the appropriate method for mounting the headboard to your bed frame or wall. Depending on your bed frame, you may need to attach mounting brackets or hooks to the back of the headboard. Employ proper wall mounting hardware if you plan to attach the headboard directly to the wall.

Step 6: Install the headboard Follow the instructions provided with the mounting brackets or hardware to attach the headboard to your bed frame or wall.

Ensure it is securely fastened and level. Congratulations! You have successfully built and installed your wooden headboard.

4. Build a birdhouse or bird feeder

Birdhouses and bird feeders are often seen as real decorations for the garden, but if they are built without due care, they can be useless or even harmful to our new guests. The most common feeders are made of wood, but they can also be made with recycled products, such as plastic. Unlike birdhouses, birds have no problems with the material with which the container is made: the important thing is that it is in a safe and protected place. Let's see how to build a bird feeder starting from a simple plastic bottle: a simple, functional and free idea.

Build a birdhouse

Here's a step-by-step guide to help you build a basic birdhouse:

Materials you'll need:

- ✓ Wood boards (3/4-inch thick, preferably untreated cedar or pine)
- ✓ Measuring tape
- ✓ Pencil
- ✓ Saw (circular saw or handsaw)
- ✓ Drill
- ✓ Drill bits (one for pilot holes and one for entry hole)
- ✓ Sandpaper (medium and fine grit)
- ✓ Exterior-grade wood glue
- ✓ Screws or nails
- ✓ Wire or twine (for hanging)
- ✓ Paint or wood stain (optional)
- ✓ Paintbrush or foam applicator (if painting or staining)

Step 1: Plan the design and dimensions.

State the size and design of your birdhouse. The dimensions and shape will be chosen based on the kind of birds you want to be there. Consider researching specific species to determine their preferred dimensions and entry hole size. A general guideline is to have a box-shaped structure with an entrance hole positioned slightly above the center.

Step 2: Cut the wood.

Using a saw, cut the wood boards into the necessary pieces according to your design. For the equipment there must be a front and back panel, two side panels, a bottom panel, and a roof panel. Remember to include the dimensions for the entrance hole.

Step 3: Drill entry and ventilation holes

Mark the location for the entrance hole on the front panel using a pencil. Employ an suitable sized drill bit to create the hole.

Step 4: Assemble the birdhouse.

Apply wood glue to the edges of the side panels and attach them to the front panel. Then add the back panel to the side panels employing screws or nails. Finally, attach the bottom panel to the assembled structure. Ensure all the pieces are aligned properly and securely fastened.

Step 5: Add the roof.

Attach the roof panel to the top of the birdhouse using screws or nails. Be certain that it overhangs the sides slightly to provide protection from the elements.

Step 6: Sand and finish.

Use sandpaper to smooth any rough edges or surfaces of the birdhouse. This will prevent splinters and provide a neater finish. If you choose to paint, use non-toxic outdoor paint to ensure the safety of the birds.

Step 7: Install hanging wire or twine.

Attach a piece of wire or twine to the top of the birdhouse for hanging. Make sure it's securely fastened and positioned in a way that allows the birdhouse to hang freely.

Step 8: Hang the birdhouse.

Find a suitable location for your birdhouse. Ideally, it should be mounted on a sturdy pole, tree, or wall, away from predators and at a height that is appropriate for the target bird species. Hang the birdhouse using the wire or twine.

Remember to regularly clean out the birdhouse between nesting seasons to maintain hygiene.

Build a bird feeder

To build this DIY manger you will need:
- Plastic bottle.
- Awl.
- Small scissors.
- Marker.
- Two wooden ladles.
- A drawstring.

The procedure is quick and easy: first take the plastic bottle, taking care to have first removed the label and washed and dried it correctly, and with the marker, mark four points on the surface; each pair of points must be parallel and at the same height so that – once the respective holes have been made – it is possible to pass the handle of the wooden spoon through them. Pierce the points with an awl: the first two holes must be at a height of at least 1.56 inches from the bottom of the bottle, the other two at about 2.73 inches.

Using the scissors, widen the holes slightly, into which the handles of the wooden spoons will have to fit easily. Once the holes have been made, insert the two spoons: the base where the birds will rest their paws is ready!

Take the cap of the bottle and - always helping yourself with the awl - make a hole in which you will then pass the two ends of the string inside, to be fixed with a knot.

Now take out both spoons, widen the upper part of the hole opposite that of the handle by about 1 cm and put the spoons back inside the feeder. The structure is ready: with a funnel, fill the bottle with birdseed and close it with the cap. Before hanging your DIY bird feeder, make sure you choose a well-protected place, securing it to a sturdy and secure branch.

5. **Build a simple table or desk**

Materials and tools
- ✓ 1.17 inches panel per top (or two 0,58 inches thick glued panels)
- ✓ 0.70 inches panel
- ✓ Solid wood table
- ✓ Thorns
- ✓ PVA glue
- ✓ Water-based stains for wood and transparent satin varnish for interiors
- ✓ Pre-glued adhesive border

Tools: Table saw, Miter saw, Screwdriver drill, Dowel template, Brush, Roller, Carpenter's square

1 Cut the panels to size.

To start building the wooden desk, first you need to cut the panels to the right size. Attached you will find the measurements of my project, but of course I suggest you adapt them to your needs! For cuts, you can use a table saw, Once the panels have been cut to size, if they are in faced plywood or blockboard it is necessary to cover them with a pre-glued adhesive edge. Alternatively you can use solid wood, i.e. strips of wood (possibly of the same essence as the panel to be edged). To apply the pre-glued border, it is necessary to use an iron at maximum power. Instead, you can attach the solid wood using normal vinyl glue.

2 Create the side with shelves.

Having bordered all the panels, I traced the position of the shelves on the two sides. To make the shelves, I used a removable system that requires the use of a professional power tool. An easier (and much cheaper) way to achieve the same result is to use pin and barrel unions or dowelling. The latter is certainly the cheapest system.

Use a template to do the dowelling.

3 Make the easel.

Always with the pinning technique it is also possible to make the tripod: in this case, however, I advise you to use 0.39 inches diameter pins. Once all the operations have been carried out to make the joints, I sanded everything with a 180 grit. Now you can add the stand and then move on to painting.

Assemble the trestle with the pins and then smooth it.

4 Paint.

The top and the two shelves have been painted with a wenge-colored water-based dye. For the easel I instead used a blue water-based paint. I painted the sides only with the transparent finish, because I wanted to leave them the natural color of the wood: ash. I also used the same transparent varnish as a final layer on the top and shelves, after the wenge color had dried well.

Once all the components are ready, you can paint them in the color you prefer.

5 Assemble.

Once the paint has dried, it's time to assemble the easel and the side with the shelves. Next, merge the plane. Your simply desk is ready.

After the sixth chapter, let's move on to the seventh which will deal with the themes of painting and decorating your house.

PART 7: Painting and Decorating

In this chapter, readers will learn how to paint walls and furniture, install wallpaper, and create custom art pieces. The chapter also covers more advanced decorating tasks such as installing statement light fixtures and creating gallery walls.

Choosing the right paint and finishes

As for the choice of paints and finishes, we have already talked about it in detail at the end of the second chapter. For this reason, we invite you to review the homonymous paragraph.

Painting techniques and tips

Painting techniques and tips can vary depending on the medium you are working with, whether it's acrylics, oils, watercolors, or any other medium. However, there are some general techniques and tips that can be helpful for any painting style. Here are a few:

- ✓ Start with a sketch: Before you begin painting, make a rough sketch of your subject on the canvas. This will help you establish the composition and proportions before adding color.
- ✓ Employ valuable materials: buy good-high paints, brushes, and canvases. Better materials will give you better control over your paint application and enhance the longevity of your artwork.
- ✓ Understand color theory: Learn about the color wheel, color mixing, and color interactions. This knowledge will allow you to create harmonious color schemes and achieve the desired effects in your painting.
- ✓ Layering and glazing: Build your painting in layers. Start with an underpainting or base layer and gradually add more layers of paint. Additionally, glazing (applying thin transparent layers of color) can create luminosity and subtle color variations.

- ✓ Play with different brush techniques: Experiment with different brushstrokes, such as broad strokes, washes, dry brushing, stippling, and scumbling. Varying your brushwork adds visual interest and texture to your painting.
- ✓ Pay attention to values: Value refers to the lightness or darkness of a color. Understanding values is crucial for creating depth and volume in your painting. Practice observing and accurately depicting the values in your subject.
- ✓ Use a limited color palette: Limiting your color palette can help create color harmony and prevent your painting from becoming too busy. Start with a few primary colors and mix them to achieve a wide range of secondary and tertiary colors.
- ✓ Study from life: Whenever possible, paint from real-life subjects. Observing and painting from life will help you develop your observational skills and capture the subtleties of light, form, and texture.
- ✓ Take breaks and step back: It's easy to get caught up in the details of a painting. Periodically take breaks and step back to view your work from a distance.
- ✓ Practice and experiment: The more you paint, the more you'll improve. Don't be afraid to try new techniques, explore different styles, and experiment with various subjects. Painting is a journey of continuous learning and growth.

Remember, these tips are general guidelines, and each artist develops their own unique style and techniques over time. So, have fun, be patient, and enjoy the process of creating art!

Repairing and preparing walls for painting

Repairing and preparing walls for painting is a vital action to obtain a smooth and professional-looking finish. Here's a step-by-step guide on how to do it.

Gather the necessary tools and materials:

- ✓ Drop cloths or plastic sheets to preserve the floor and furniture.
- ✓ Painter's tape to mask off areas you are not going to color.
- ✓ Putty knife or scraper to remove loose paint or wallpaper.
- ✓ Sandpaper (medium and fine grit) or sanding block.
- ✓ Patching compound or spackling paste.
- ✓ Primer.
- ✓ Paintbrushes and rollers.
- ✓ Paint.

Clear the room.

Remove furniture, wall decorations, and switch covers to create a clear workspace. Cover the floor and any remaining furniture through drop cloths or plastic sheets to preserve these items and avoid to dust and paint splatters.

Prepare the walls.

Remove any loose or peeling paint using a putty knife or scraper. Scrape gently to avoid damaging the underlying surface.

If there are holes or cracks in the wall, use patching compound or spackling paste to fill them.

Apply the compound with a putty knife and let it dry.

Once the compound is dry, sand the patched areas using medium-grit sandpaper or a sanding block. This will create a smooth surface and blend the patched areas with the rest of the wall.

After sanding, wipe the walls through a damp cloth or sponge to eliminate any dust or debris.

Apply primer.

Priming the walls could be essential because you are protecting a repaired area. Primer can be useful to make the paint more adherent and gives a consistent base color.

So, you can employ a paintbrush to apply primer around the edges and corners, and a roller for wider areas.

Let the primer dry completely before going to the next step.

Paint the walls.

Once the primer is dry, you can keep the project by painting the walls. Choose the desired paint color and finish (matte, satin, semi-gloss, etc.).

You can do, as first step, a cutting in the edges with a paintbrush, painting along the corners, ceiling, and baseboards.

Employ a roller to paint the larger wall areas. Work in small sections, applying the paint in a "W" or "M" pattern, and then roll vertically from top to bottom for an even application.

Remove the painter's tape while the final coat is still slightly wet to prevent peeling.

Clean up.

Once you've finished painting, clean all the tools you have properly used.

Remove the drop cloths or plastic sheets and put the furniture and decorations back in place.

Remember to take your time and allow each step to dry properly before moving on to the next one.

Installing wallpaper or wall coverings

Installing wallpaper and wall coverings can be a great way to enhance the look of a room and add a personal touch to your living space. Here's a step-by-step guide to help you with the installation process:

Set the wall: Start by setting properly the wall surface. Remove any existing wallpaper, loose paint, or debris. Make sure the wall is clean and dry before proceeding.

Measure and cut: As first step take both the height and width measures of the wall you're planning to cover. Add a few inches to each measurement to account for trimming and adjustments. Use these measurements to cut the wallpaper or wall covering panels accordingly.

Mix adhesive (if required): Some wallpapers require adhesive, while others come with a peel-and-stick backing. If your wallpaper needs adhesive, mix it according to the manufacturer's instructions. Use a wallpaper paste or adhesive recommended for the specific type of wallpaper you're installing.

Apply adhesive or peel off backing: If using adhesive, apply it to the back of the wallpaper evenly, using a paint roller or brush. Be certain of covering the entire surface but avoid excessive application. If you're using peel-and-stick wallpaper, simply peel off the backing.

Hang the first panel: Starting from a corner or the center of the wall, carefully align the top of the wallpaper panel with the ceiling or a level guideline. Smooth the wallpaper from top to bottom, ensuring there are no air bubbles or wrinkles. Use a wallpaper brush or a plastic smoothing tool to remove any imperfections and ensure proper adhesion.

Continue hanging panels: Align the subsequent panels with each other, matching patterns if applicable. Overlap the edges slightly but avoid overlapping too much to prevent visible seams. Smooth out each panel as you go, ensuring a seamless appearance.

Trim excess wallpaper: Once all the panels are hung, use a sharp utility knife or wallpaper trimming tool to cut off the excess at the ceiling, baseboards, and corners. Take care not to damage the wall surface while trimming.

Repeat for additional walls: If you're covering multiple walls, repeat the above steps for each wall, starting from the same corner or center point.

Finishing touches: Once the wallpaper is installed, go over the entire surface to ensure it is smooth and properly adhered. Eliminate any excess adhesive with a damp sponge or cloth. Allow the wallpaper to dry completely according to the manufacturer's instructions.

Remember to read and follow the specific instructions provided by the manufacturer of your wallpaper or wall covering, as different products may have variations in installation techniques.

A painting step-by-step project

Here you are a painting step by step project.

Refinish a piece of furniture

As first step, you should remove stains. The halo of a cup or glass is one of the most common stains, fortunately getting rid of it is not difficult:

- Apply a few drops of straw oil.
- Use a very fine abrasive to gently sand the wood.
- Finish by spreading the shellac.
- Put on latex gloves and create a tampon by dipping the wool in shellac, then wring it out well and wrap it in an old rag. Finally, swab the wood.
- Rebuild missing parts/remove scratches-holes-cracks.

A piece of furniture with holes or cracks can return to its former glory:

- Apply an anti-woodworm product.
- Wear gloves and spread the ready-to-use filler, first on the missing parts, then inside all the cracks, finally in the scratches and holes (if you love the vintage effect, you can avoid filling everything and leave some signs of ageing).
- Sand the wood to remove the filler.
- If necessary, touch up the grout with wax.
- Wipe with a cloth moistened with alcohol to remove dust and stains.
- Apply a water-based dye, the same shade as the wood, using a piece of foam rubber.
- Spread the shellac with the brush and let it dry.
- Pass the steel wool to make the wood smoother and softer.
- Spread the shellac with the wool pad (if you like a more rustic finish, you can use a solid wax the same color as the wood instead of shellac).

Install crown molding

Installing crown molding can be a great way to add elegance and visual interest to your home. Here's a general guide to help you get started with the installation process:

Take the necessary equipment:
- Crown molding
- Measuring tape
- Miter saw
- Coping saw
- Nail gun or hammer and finishing nails
- Wood filler
- Sandpaper
- Caulk
- Paint or stain (if desired)

Measure and plan:

Take the length of each wall where you intend to mount crown molding.

Determine the type and size of crown molding you want to use.

Calculate the amount of molding needed by adding up the lengths of the walls and adding a little extra for waste.

Cut the crown molding:

Use a miter saw to cut the first piece of molding at a 90-degree angle (straight cut) according to the wall length.

Split the next piece at a 45-degree angle, but in the opposite direction, so it will fit against the first piece. This is called a mitered cut.

For inside corners, cut the molding at a 45-degree angle in the same direction as the first piece.

For outside corners, cut the molding at a 45-degree angle in the opposite direction of the first piece.

If there are complex corners or uneven walls, you may need to use a coping saw to shape the ends of the molding to fit perfectly.

Install the crown molding:

Start with one wall and apply a thin line of adhesive caulk along the back of the molding.

Press the molding firmly against the wall and use a nail gun or hammer and finishing nails to secure it in place. Place nails at the top and bottom of the molding, aiming for studs if possible.

Continue this process for the remaining walls, ensuring that each piece is properly aligned and mitered at the corners.

Employ some wood filler to fill in any nail holes in the joints.

Sand the molding lightly to smooth out any rough edges.

Apply caulk along the seams between the molding and the wall, as well as any gaps or joints, to create a seamless look.

Finishing touches:

If desired, paint or stain the crown molding to match your room's decor.

Clean up any excess caulk, paint, or stain for a polished finish.

Paint or stain kitchen cabinets

Painting or staining kitchen cabinets can be a proper solution to give your kitchen a fresh, and amazing look. Deciding between painting or staining kitchen cabinets is a matter of personal preference and the desired aesthetic for your kitchen.

Below we will provide you some steps to help you through the actions:

Preparation:

Remove all cabinet doors, drawers, and hardware (such as handles and hinges).

Clean the surfaces thoroughly using a mild detergent and warm water to remove grease, grime, and any residue.

Wipe away any dust with a tack cloth.

Painting:

If you opt for painting, start by applying a coat of primer to the cabinet surfaces. This helps the paint adhere better and provides a smooth base.

Once the primer is dry, apply thin, even coats of paint using a brush or roller. You can employ, in this case, a paint sprayer for reaching a professional finish.

Allow each coat to dry completely before applying the next one. Multiple thin coats are better than one thick coat.

Pay attention to details, such as edges and corners, to obtain a full coverage.

After the final coat, let the paint cure before reattaching the hardware and reinstalling the cabinet doors.

Staining:

If you prefer staining, begin by applying the wood stain using a brush or cloth, following the wood grain.

Wipe off any excess stain with a clean cloth after a few minutes. The longer the stain sits, the darker the result will be, so test it on a small, inconspicuous area first to achieve your desired color.

Let the stain dry between coats. Add additional coats for a deeper color, if desired.

After the final coat, apply a protective clear coat or sealer to safeguard the finish.

Once everything is dry, reattach the hardware and reinstall the cabinet doors.

Remember, always work in a well-ventilated area and follow the instructions and safety precautions provided by the paint or stain manufacturer. Proper preparation and attention to detail will ensure a successful outcome for your kitchen cabinets.

Paint or stain a front door

Painting or staining a front door is a great way to enhance its appearance and protect it from the elements. The process involves several steps, which I'll outline below:

Preparation:

The first step is removing the door from its hinges, if possible. If removing the door is not feasible, you can cover the surrounding areas with drop cloths or painter's tape to protect them from accidental spills.

Clean the door thoroughly using a mild detergent or a mixture of water and vinegar. This operation makes quite sure the fact that the surface will be totally free from dirt, dust, and any previous finishes.

Sanding:

If the door has an existing paint or stain finish, you'll need to sand it down to create a smooth surface for the new finish. Use medium-grit sandpaper (around 120-grit) to remove the old finish. Sand in the direction of the wood grain and be certain of sanding any intricate areas or details on the door.

Repair and Patching:

Inspect the door for any cracks, holes, or imperfections. Fill these with a suitable wood filler and allow it to dry. Once dry, sand the filled areas lightly to ensure a flush surface.

Priming:

Applying a primer can be really useful for more paint or stain adhering and gives a consistent base color. Choose a primer suitable for your chosen finish (paint or stain) and apply it evenly to the door's surface. Follow the manufacturer's instructions for drying time.

Painting:

If you decide to paint the door, choose a high-quality exterior paint designed for doors and trim. Select the desired color and apply thin, even coats using a brush or a roller. Let every coat dry before applying the next one and follow the manufacturer's recommendations regarding drying time.

Staining:

If you prefer to stain the door, choose a suitable exterior wood stain. Put the stain evenly employing a brush or a rag, following the wood grain direction. Allow the stain to penetrate the wood for the recommended duration specified by the manufacturer. Remove any excess stain with a clean cloth.

Finishing:

Once the paint or stain has dried completely, you can consider applying a clear topcoat for added protection.

Reinstallation:

After the finish has fully cured, reattach the door to its hinges and make any required adjustments to ensure some right alignment and operation.

Remember to consult the specific product instructions for the paint or stain you're using, as different brands may have slightly different application methods and drying times. Additionally, ensure you work in a well-ventilated area and take appropriate safety precautions, such as wearing protective gloves and a mask, when working with paints, stains, or chemical substances.

Install a statement light fixture

Installing a statement light fixture can be a great way to enhance the aesthetics of a room. So, we will provide you general guide on how to install a light fixture:

Ensure safety: Before starting any electrical work, be certain of having turn off the power supply to the area you'll be working in. Place the circuit breaker that controls the power to the existing light fixture and turn it off.

Gather tools and materials: You'll need a few tools and materials for the installation:

New statement light fixture

Screwdriver

Wire connectors

Ladder or step stool (if needed)

Electrical tape.

Remove the existing fixture: Unscrew and take away the old light fixture from the ceiling. Take note of the wires and how they are joint. Carefully disconnect the wires from the fixture, making sure to cap the ends with wire connectors or electrical tape to prevent any accidental contact.

Prepare the new fixture: Read the installation instructions provided with your new statement light fixture. Assemble any components according to the manufacturer's instructions, such as attaching mounting brackets or adjusting the chain length.

Connect the wiring:

Begin by identifying the wires in the ceiling. Put together the wires from the ceiling to the corresponding wires on the new fixture. Most modern fixtures have color-coded wires to help with this process. Connect the black wires, the white wires, and the ground wires together using wire connectors, ensuring a secure and tight connection.

Tuck the connected wires into the electrical box in the ceiling, making sure they are not pinched or strained.

Mount the fixture: Follow the manufacturer's instructions to attach the statement light fixture to the ceiling. This may involve securing a mounting bracket, attaching the fixture with screws, or other specific instructions based on the design.

Double-check connections: Before turning the power back on, inspect the wiring connections to be certain of the fact that they are secure and there are no exposed wires. Give the fixture a gentle tug to ensure it is firmly attached to the ceiling.

Restore power and test: Go back to the circuit breaker panel and turn on the power to the area. Return to the newly installed fixture and test it by flipping the switch. If the light functions properly, you have successfully installed your statement light fixture.

Add decorative tile to a backsplash or fireplace

Below there is step-by-step guide on how you can go about it:

Plan and Design:

Determine the style and color scheme you desire for your tiles. Consider the existing decor and aesthetic of the room to ensure harmony.

Measure the area where you want to install the tile, whether it's the backsplash or fireplace surround, to determine the quantity of tiles you'll need.

Choose the Tiles:

Visit a local tile showroom or browse online to explore various options. Consider factors like material, shape, size, color, and pattern.

For a backsplash, ceramic, porcelain, or glass tiles are normally employed because of their durability and ease of maintenance.

For a fireplace, natural stone tiles like marble, slate, or travertine can create an elegant and timeless look.

Set the Surface:

Be certain of the surface where you'll be placing the tiles is clean, dry, and smooth. If necessary, remove any existing tiles, wallpaper, or debris.

Repair any cracks or imperfections in the wall or fireplace surface.

Gather the Tools and Materials:

Depending on the type of tile and the installation method, you may need tools such as a tile cutter, notched trowel, adhesive, grout, spacers, level, and sponge.

Buy all the necessary materials depending on your tile selection and the manufacturer's recommendations.

Install the Tile:

Apply adhesive to the wall or fireplace surface using a notched trowel. Start from the bottom and work your way up.

Press the tiles into the adhesive, using spacers to keep consistent grout lines. Check the level frequently to ensure evenness.

Trim tiles as needed to fit the edges or corners of the area.

Let the adhesive dry before moving on to grouting.

Grout the Tiles:

Mix the grout.

Employ a grout float to place the grout over the tiles, pressing it into the gaps among them at a 45-degree angle.

Wipe off excess grout with a damp sponge before it dries, being careful not to remove grout from the gaps.

Remember to follow the specific instructions provided by the manufacturer for the tile adhesive and grout you choose, as they may have variations in application and curing times.

With these steps, you'll be well on your way to adding decorative tile to your space, including a beautiful backsplash and fireplace surround.

In the next chapter the main topic will be outdoor home improvements.

PART 8: Outdoor Improvements

This chapter covers a variety of outdoor improvement projects, including building raised garden beds, installing patios and decks, and creating outdoor seating areas. The chapter also covers more advanced projects like building outdoor kitchens and installing water features.

Landscaping and garden design

Landscaping and garden design involve the planning, arrangement, and organization of outdoor spaces to create functional and aesthetically pleasing environments. It combines elements such as plants, trees, shrubs, hardscape features, water features, and various design principles to transform outdoor areas into beautiful and functional spaces.

Below we will show you some key aspects of landscaping and garden design:

Site Analysis: Assess the characteristics of the site, including its size, topography, soil conditions, and climate. Understanding these factors will help determine the suitability of different plants and design features for the space.

Design Principles: Apply design principles such as balance, unity, proportion, rhythm, and focal points to create a visually appealing and harmonious garden. Consider factors like color, texture, form, and scale when selecting plants and materials.

Plant choosing opt for some plants that are adapt for the local climate and site conditions. Consider factors like sun exposure, soil type, water requirements, and maintenance needs. Incorporate a variety of plants to create interest and diversity in the garden.

Hardscape Elements: Include hardscape features like pathways, patios, decks, walls, and fences to provide structure, define spaces, and add functionality to the garden. Choose materials that complement the overall design and are adaptable for the proper use.

Water Features: Incorporate water elements such as ponds, fountains, or waterfalls to add tranquility and visual interest. Consider the sound, movement, and reflection of water to create a relaxing atmosphere.

Lighting: Plan for appropriate lighting to enhance the garden's aesthetics and functionality during the evening or nighttime. Use a combination of ambient, task, and accent lighting to highlight key features, improve safety, and create a desired mood.

Maintenance: Design the garden with maintenance requirements in mind. Choose plants and materials that are manageable and suited to the available time and resources for upkeep. Proper maintenance ensures the long-term health and beauty of the landscape.

Remember, landscaping and garden design are highly creative and personal processes. It's important to consider your preferences, needs, and the overall functionality of the outdoor space when designing your garden.

Installing a new patio or deck

Let's see how to install a new patio or deck. While different insulated patio cover kits have specific installation instructions, the process usually follows the same general procedures to achieve a cover that will support the elements without damaging your home. Things you will need

- Ladders
- insulated patio cover kit
- Construction sticker
- Electric screwdriver or electric drill with an attached screwdriver
- Masonry screws
- Clamps
- Tape measure
- Pressure treated 4-by - 4 lumber.

Up a ladder near the site of your patio cover installation. Examine the eaves under your home's roof and the fascia of the wall to determine an appropriate place to install the header, which is the horizontal bar that attaches an insulated patio cover to your home.

Choose a site that is sturdy and relatively smooth.

Apply the construction adhesive to the back of the headboard that comes in the insulated patio roofing kit using a brush or applicator that comes with the adhesive.

Press the header against the installation site. Drive screws through it, into masonry or wood studs on your home's exterior, using an electric screwdriver or drill with a screwdriver bit. Employ the masonry screws in place of the screws provided in the cover kit. Lock the header in place, if possible, using metal ties. Wait for the construction adhesive to dry according to the manufacturer's suggested cure times for the current temperature and humidity level.

Attach the mounting brackets to the insulated patio cover header with the screws provided and a power screwdriver or power drill with a screwdriver bit.

Attach the concrete brackets to the patio floor where the posts will rise. There's no need to dig handholds if your insulated patio cover will be supported by a header attached to your house.

Insert and screw ordered 4-by-4 lumber of a length that matches the height of your posts into the concrete brackets. Insert and screw together the remaining frame pieces of the patio cover kit, connecting the posts to the header and to each other at their tops.

Install the insulated patio cover panels by snapping or screwing them into place, following the installation instructions that come with the kit.

Adding a pool or hot tub

Adding a pool and hot tub to your home can be a wonderful choice to improving your outdoor space and provide a relaxing and enjoyable experience. Below you can find some considerations and steps to help you in this project:

Design and Planning, so determine the available space: Assess the available area in your yard to determine the suitable size and location for the pool and hot tub.

Research local regulations: Check with your local municipality or homeowners' association for any permits or regulations regarding the installation of pools and hot tubs.

Choose the type and style: Decide whether you want an in-ground pool, an above-ground pool, or a portable pool. Consider the various types of hot tubs available and select one that fits your preferences.

Plan the surrounding area: Think about the landscaping, seating, and any additional features you want to incorporate around the pool and hot tub.

Hiring Professionals:

Pool contractor: Hire a reputable pool contractor who specializes in pool installations. They will guide you through the process, assist with design, and handle the construction.

Electrician: Engage a qualified electrician to install the necessary electrical connections for the pool and hot tub.

Permits and Inspections:

Obtain permits: Apply for the required permits as per local regulations. Your pool contractor can assist you with this process.

Schedule inspections: Arrange for the necessary inspections during different stages of the installation to ensure compliance with safety standards.

Construction and Installation:

Excavation: The pool contractor will excavate the designated area to create the space for the pool and hot tub.

Pool installation: Depending on your chosen pool type, the contractor will construct the pool structure, install the filtration system, and connect the necessary plumbing.

Hot tub installation:

If you opted for an above ground or portable hot tub, follow the manufacturer's instructions for installation. For in-ground hot tubs, the pool contractor can integrate it into the design during the pool construction process.

Landscaping and Finishing Touches:

Surrounding area: Work on the landscaping around the pool and hot tub, including features like decking, patio, plants, or seating areas.

Safety measures: Install safety features such as fences, gates, or pool covers to ensure the security of children and pets.

Lighting and accessories: Consider adding lighting features, outdoor furniture, and other accessories to create a welcoming and enjoyable atmosphere.

Remember to consult with professionals throughout the process to ensure a safe and successful installation.

Repairing or replacing your roof

Repairing and replacing a roof can be a significant undertaking, but it is essential for maintaining the integrity and safety of your home. Here are some general steps and considerations to keep in mind when it comes to repairing or replacing a roof:

Assess the condition: Start by inspecting your roof to determine whether it needs repair or replacement. Seek for damage aspects, like missing or cracked shingles, leaks, sagging areas, or visible wear and tear. If the damage is localized and minor, repairs may be sufficient.

Safety first: roof can be dangerous, so prioritize safety.

Obtain permits and approvals: based on your living place and the extent of the work, you may need to get permits or approvals from local authorities. So, keep in touch with your local building department to ensure you comply with any necessary regulations.

Get multiple quotes: If you decide to hire a professional roofing contractor, obtain quotes from several reputable companies. Compare their prices, expertise, warranties, and customer reviews to make an informed decision.

Choose roofing materials: If you're replacing the entire roof, consider the various roofing materials available, such as asphalt shingles, metal, tile, or wood shakes. Select a material that suits your budget and needs.

Schedule the work: Coordinate with the roofing contractor to set a timeline for the project. Keep in mind that weather conditions can affect the schedule, so plan accordingly.

Prepare the site: Before the work begins, clear the area that surround your home to ensure a simpler access for the roofing crew. Move vehicles, outdoor furniture, and other obstacles that may hinder the project.

Repair or replace: Depending on the assessment, the contractor will either repair or replace the roof. Repairs may involve fixing damaged shingles, sealing leaks, or addressing localized issues. In the case of a replacement, the old roofing materials are removed, and new ones are installed following the appropriate techniques and industry standards.

Clean up and inspection: Once the work is completed, the contractor should clean up the job site, removing debris and ensuring your property is left in good condition. A final inspection should also be conducted to verify that the roof repairs or replacement meet the required standards.

Outdoor improvement step-by-step projects

Here some home outdoor improvement step-by step projects.

Build a raised garden bed

Raised flower beds are certainly an enrichment for your garden. Here are the various steps to make it happen.

Step 1 - The right preparations for setting up the raised bed.

The best times to set up a raised flower bed are autumn and early spring. But the months of February and March are also good, since in this period you have a lot of organic waste from the garden and garden and compost that you can use to fill the flower bed.

Before getting to work, you need to decide which material to build the perimeter structure of the flowerbed with. Wood is easy to work with and is pleasing to the eye, but over time it needs more intensive care than a stone bed. Wood should be pre-treated to reduce the effects of weathering. By using a more durable type of wood like Douglas fir you can minimize maintenance.

Finally, the metal is durable over time, but in terms of insulation and heat storage, it leaves much to be desired.

Step 2 - Build the supporting structure of the raised bed.

Once you have chosen the material in which to build the perimeter structure of the raised flower bed, select a sunny place to install it and plan its construction with the long sides facing north south. The best exposure to sunlight will in fact promote rigorous growth of your plants. Have you chosen to use a wooden structure? Then mount the boards with set squares and screws. A cordless screwdriver will allow you to be faster.

If, on the other hand, you want to build it in bricks, raise a masonry to the height you want.

First prepare a solid gravel foundation and start by lining up a first row of common bricks. Then continue with the clinker bricks and mortar until you reach a height of 31.2 inches.

Lay a fine-mesh wire mesh over the bottom of the flower bed to keep moles and rodents out.

The raised masonry flower bed must be covered inside with a shaped panel to protect the walls from excessive humidity.

Step 3 - Fix a shaped panel inside the flower bed.

To prevent moisture damage to plants and the perimeter structure, line the inside walls of the flowerbed with a shaped panel or pond liner. To facilitate the following phases, mark on the shaped covering the height of the different layers that you will gradually insert inside the flowerbed.

The gardener inserts the lowest layer in the masonry structure of the raised flower bed: coarse pruning and wood chips,

Step 4 - Fill the bed layer by layer.

Fill the base of the flowerbed with a layer of branches and coarse pruning to a height of about 20 cm, placing it on the wire mesh. To do this, use a pitchfork. On top of it lay some sod with the grass side down and compact them well.

The third layer of 7.8 inches consists of wet foliage in an initial state of decomposition and organic waste. The fourth layer follows, a coarse and not yet matured compost. In another point of view, you can also employ decomposed animal manure. Finally, spread a 9.75 inches layer of soil mixed with humus and mature compost. The different layers that form the raised bed are shown in the table below. Renew the contents of the flowerbed every 5 years.

1st layer

wood chips (shredded branch pruning) and garden waste

2nd layer

upside down turf

3rd layer

foliage and organic matter in an initial state of decomposition

4th layer

coarse compost or manure

5th layer

loam mixed with humus and mature compost.

Step 5 - Plant the plants

The different layers of organic material decompose, releasing precious humus rich in nutrients and heat. For this reason, the temperature inside the raised beds is generally about 5 degrees higher than that of the beds lying on the ground and the harvest goes on into late autumn.

In the first two years of planting, the raised beds offer very rich nourishment. Take advantage of it by growing plants that require an abundant supply of nutrients, such as peppers, tomatoes and leeks. For the rest, it's up to you to choose what to plant in your raised bed: vegetables, herbs or flowers.

Install a patio or deck

See above the installing procedure.

Build an outdoor kitchen or grill station

Building an outdoor kitchen grill station can be a fun and rewarding project. You can star by:

Design and Planning:

Determine the size and layout of your grill station. Consider factors such as available space, your cooking needs, and any local regulations or restrictions.

Opt for the materials you want to employ, like stone, brick, concrete, or metal. Be sure that they are proper for outdoor use and can withstand heat and weather conditions.

Gather Materials and Tools:

Purchase the necessary materials based on your design. This may include bricks, concrete blocks, mortar, cement, gravel, rebar, grill components, countertop materials, and any other accessories you want to include.

Gather tools such as a shovel, wheelbarrow, level, tape measure, masonry trowel, rubber mallet, masonry saw, and safety equipment.

Set the Site:

Clear the area where you plan to build the grill station. Remove any vegetation, rocks, or debris.

Level the ground using a shovel and a rake. You may need to remove or add soil to obtain a flat and stable surface.

Build the Base:

Lay the foundation for your grill station using concrete or concrete blocks.

If using concrete blocks, stack them according to your desired height, making sure to apply mortar between each layer.

Construct the Grill Structure:

Use bricks, concrete blocks, or other chosen materials to build the walls and structure of the grill station. Follow your design plan and use mortar to secure the pieces together.

Consider leaving spaces for storage compartments or shelving if desired.

Install Countertops and Surfaces:

Add a countertop or work surface next to the grill for your preparations. Materials such as granite, stainless steel, or tile work well for outdoor use.

Ensure that the surface is level and securely attached to the grill structure.

Install the Grill and Accessories:

Follow the manufacturer's instructions to install your chosen grill and any additional accessories, such as burners, side tables, or storage cabinets.

Make sure to connect gas lines or install any required ventilation systems according to local codes and safety guidelines.

Finishing Touches:

Clean the grill station and remove any construction debris.

Consider adding finishing touches like a backsplash, lighting, seating, or decorative elements to enhance the aesthetics of your outdoor grill station.

Always prioritize safety when working with tools, materials, and open flames.

Install a water feature or fountain

Installing a water feature and fountain can add beauty and quietly to your space. Here are the general steps to install a water feature and fountain:

Plan and design: Determine the location and type of water feature and fountain you want. Take into account elements such as the size, style, and materials that will complement your space. Also, check local regulations or homeowner association rules regarding water features.

Gather materials: Purchase the necessary materials, which may include a water pump, tubing, basin or reservoir, decorative stones or pebbles, and any additional accessories or lighting you desire.

Set the site: Clear the area where you are going to place the water feature and fountain. Ensure the ground is level and stable. If necessary, excavate the area or build a foundation for the fountain.

Install the reservoir or basin: Place the reservoir or basin in the desired location. It should be large enough to hold the water and accommodate the pump.

Install the pump: Connect the tubing to the pump's outlet.

Arrange the water feature elements: Set up any decorative elements such as rocks, pebbles, or sculptures around the water feature to enhance its appearance.

Connect the tubing: Attach the other end of the tubing to the water feature, ensuring a secure and watertight connection. Position the water feature in or above the reservoir, allowing the water to flow back into the basin.

Fill the reservoir: Fill the reservoir with water, ensuring the pump is fully submerged.

Test the system: Turn on the pump to test the water flow and make any necessary adjustments to achieve the desired effect. Look for leaks and be certain that the water is circulating properly.

Final touches: Once you are satisfied with the water feature's installation and functionality, add any final touches, such as adjusting the decorative elements, adding lighting, or integrating the fountain with your existing landscaping.

Remember to follow all safety guidelines and electrical codes when working with water and electricity.

Install a pergola or gazebo

In general, we know that the installation of a pergola or a gazebo if it is easily removable, without a fixed cover and free on at least 3 sides does not require a building permit. If, on the other hand, it is even partially surmounted by a roof in rigid material, it is equated to a canopy. For the latter, the PDC is mandatory, as it is a stable and not precarious work.

Before installing the pergola, check that the ground is stable. The legs of the pergola or for a gazebo must be screwed or sealed into the ground. Since the structure is relatively large, at least two people are required for assembly. Some of the lighter arbors, intended to be temporary, can simply be screwed in or pegged down.

Collapsible gazebos must not be fixed to the ground. More convenient, they allow you to create a shelter during family events, but it is not recommended to keep them outside all year round.

Build a treehouse or playset

Building a treehouse and playset can provide a fun and adventurous space for children. Below you will find general outline of the actions involved in constructing a treehouse and playset:

Design and plan: Determine the size, style, and features of your treehouse and playset. Take measurements of the selected tree or area where you intend to build.

Obtain necessary permissions: Check local regulations and obtain any required permits or permissions for building a treehouse and playset in your area. Some jurisdictions may have specific rules regarding height, safety, and structures built on trees.

Gather materials and tools: Prepare a list of materials needed based on your design. This may consider lumber, screws, nails, brackets, swing sets, slides, and other accessories.

Prepare the site: Clear the area where you plan to build the treehouse and playset. Remove any obstacles, rocks, or debris. If constructing a treehouse, evaluate the health and stability of the tree. Consult an arborist if needed to ensure the tree can support the structure.

Build the foundation: Construct a solid and level foundation for the treehouse or playset. This could involve building a platform with beams and joists. If using a tree, consider using special brackets or hardware designed for treehouse construction to minimize damage to the tree.

Frame the structure: Build the walls, floor, and roof of the treehouse according to your design. Use sturdy lumber and secure the structure with appropriate screws or nails. Follow construction best practices for safety and stability.

Install safety features: Incorporate safety measures such as handrails, guardrails, and netting where necessary to prevent falls and accidents. Ensure that all materials used meet safety standards.

Add the playset elements: If including a playset, install swings, slides, climbing walls, or any other desired features.

Finish and decorate: Apply a weather-resistant finish to the treehouse and playset to protect the wood from the elements. Consider adding decorative elements such as paint, flags, or themed accessories to enhance the play area.

Test and inspect: Before allowing children to use the treehouse and playset, thoroughly inspect the structure for any loose components, sharp edges, or potential hazards. Test all equipment for proper functioning.

Remember to prioritize safety throughout the construction process and ensure that the structure is well-built and sturdy.

Ended these eight chapters, in the next one will be explained all about home renovations.

PART 9: Renovations

In this chapter, readers will learn how to tackle major renovation projects such as installing new kitchen countertops, refinishing cabinets, and finishing a basement into a new living space.

Kitchen remodeling

Kitchen remodeling is the process of renovating or making improvements to a kitchen to provide it more functionality, aesthetics, without forgetting a higher value. It involves making changes to various aspects of the kitchen, such as the layout, cabinets, countertops, appliances, flooring, lighting, and plumbing fixtures. Let's see all the steps for a kitchen remodeling project:

Planning and design: Determine your goals and objectives for the remodel. Think about elements such as your budget, desired style, and functional needs. Create a detailed plan and layout for the new kitchen design, considering factors such as the work triangle (the distance between the sink, stove, and refrigerator) and proper space utilization.

Budgeting: state a budget for your kitchen remodel. Look for the costs linked to the materials, work, and any additional expenses. It's important to have a clear idea of what you can afford and prioritize your spending accordingly.

Demolition and construction: If major structural changes are required, such as removing walls or relocating plumbing or electrical systems, this is the time to do it. Demolish the existing kitchen components and begin the construction phase. This may involve framing, drywall installation, flooring, and any necessary structural modifications.

Plumbing and electrical work: Install or modify plumbing and electrical systems as per the new kitchen layout. This includes relocating water and gas lines, installing new fixtures, outlets, switches, and lighting fixtures.

Install new cabinets, countertops, and appliances based on the design plan. Choose high-quality materials that suit your style and functional requirements. Coordinate with contractors and suppliers to ensure proper installation and integration of these items.

Flooring and backsplash: Install new flooring materials, such as hardwood, tile, or laminate, based on your preference. Additionally, install a backsplash to protect the walls from splashes and enhance the visual appeal. There are various materials available, including tiles, stone, glass, or metal.

Finishing touches: Complete the remodel by adding finishing touches, such as painting the walls, installing light fixtures, and adding decorative elements. Pay attention to details like trim, hardware, and accessories to tie the entire kitchen together.

Bathroom remodeling

Bathroom remodeling is the action of renovating or improving a bathroom to amplify its functionality, aesthetics, and value. It involves making changes to various aspects of the bathroom, including the layout, fixtures, finishes, storage, and lighting. Here you are what you can do for a bathroom remodeling project:

Planning and design: Determine your goals and objectives for the remodel. Consider factors like your budget, desired style, and functional needs. Create a detailed plan and layout for the new bathroom design, considering the existing plumbing and electrical configurations.

Budgeting: state a budget for your bathroom remodel. Like the kitchen one, it's essential to have a clear idea of what you can afford and prioritize your spending accordingly.

Demolition and construction: Clear out the existing bathroom fixtures and materials to make way for the new design. This may involve removing old tiles, flooring, cabinets, fixtures, and walls if necessary. Ensure that proper safety measures are in place during the demolition process.

Plumbing and electrical work: If you're making changes to the plumbing or electrical systems, this is the time to do it. Relocate or install new pipes, drains, and fixtures as per the new bathroom layout. Similarly, modify or upgrade electrical wiring, outlets, switches, and lighting fixtures.

Flooring and wall finishes: Install new flooring materials such as tiles, vinyl, or hardwood, based on your preferences and budget. Apply wall finishes such as paint, wallpaper, or tile. Be certain of the materials you have chosen are suitable for wet environments and are simple to clean and maintain.

Fixtures and cabinetry: Install new fixtures like sinks, bathtubs, toilets, showers and faucets. Select high-quality fixtures that match your design style and functional needs. Install cabinets or storage units for increased organization and functionality.

Lighting and ventilation: Upgrade or install new lighting fixtures to improve the overall ambiance and functionality of the bathroom. Install or upgrade ventilation systems to avoid moisture buildup and provide more air circulation.

Finishing touches: Complete the remodel by adding finishing touches, such as installing mirrors, towel racks, hooks, and other accessories. Pay attention to details like trim, hardware, and decor to tie the entire bathroom together.

Basement finishing

Basement finishing refers to the process of renovating or remodeling the basement area of a home to make it a functional and livable space. A finished basement can serve various purposes, such as providing additional living space, creating an entertainment area, setting up a home office, or adding extra bedrooms or bathrooms. Here are some general steps and considerations involved in finishing a basement:

Plan and Design: establish how you with to employ the space and set a detailed plan. Consider factors like the layout, lighting, ventilation, and any necessary permits or building codes.

Moisture Control: Basements are prone to moisture issues, so it's crucial to address any existing water problems or potential risks. Install proper insulation, waterproofing, and drainage systems to avoid leaks and moisture buildup.

Framing: Build the framework for walls, partitions, and any necessary structural elements. Use treated lumber or metal studs to protect from moisture and potential mold growth.

Electrical and Plumbing: Install or extend electrical wiring and outlets to accommodate your desired lighting, appliances, and electronics.

Insulation: Install insulation between the walls, floors, and ceilings to improve energy efficiency and soundproofing. Choose the appropriate type of insulation based on your local climate and building codes.

Walls and Ceilings: Install drywall or other suitable wall materials and finish them with paint or wallpaper. Consider using moisture-resistant drywall in areas prone to dampness. For the ceiling, options include drywall, suspended ceiling tiles, or exposed beams.

Flooring: Choose a flooring material that suits your needs and budget. Popular options for basements include carpet, laminate, engineered wood, vinyl, or tile. Ensure the flooring is suitable for below-grade installations and provides proper insulation.

Lighting: Plan the lighting layout to obtain a well-lit and suitable space. Utilize a combination of ambient, task, and accent lighting to suit different activities and enhance the atmosphere.

Heating and Cooling: Extend the existing HVAC (heating, ventilation, and air conditioning) system to the basement or consider alternative heating and cooling options, such as radiant floor heating or mini-split systems.

Finishing Touches: Add the final touches to obtain a working and aesthetically pleasing space. This includes installing doors, trim, baseboards, and any desired built-in shelving or storage solutions.

Remember to consult local building codes, obtain necessary permits, and consider hiring professionals for certain tasks, especially if you lack the required expertise.

Adding an addition to your home

Adding an addition to your home is a significant project that can provide more living space and expand the value of your property. Here are some steps and considerations to check when planning an addition:

Determine Your Needs: Identify why you want to add an addition to your home. Do you need extra bedrooms, a larger living area, a home office, or a new space for a specific purpose? Understanding your needs will help guide the design process.

Assess Feasibility: Consider the available space on your property and evaluate if there are any zoning restrictions or building codes that may impact the addition.

Design and Plan: Ensure that the design blends seamlessly with the architectural style of your house.

Consider Structural Integrity: Assess if your existing foundation and structure can support the addition. A structural engineer can evaluate this and provide recommendations if any modifications are necessary.

Set a Budget: set your budget for the addition, including construction costs, permits, and any additional cost such as furniture or landscaping.

Construction: The construction project will involve several stages, like excavation, foundation work, roofing, framing, electrical and plumbing installations, insulation, drywall, flooring, and final touches. Hire licensed contractors for each phase and schedule regular inspections to ensure compliance with building codes.

Connect Utilities: If your addition requires additional electrical, plumbing, or HVAC systems, work with professionals to connect them to your existing utilities. This may involve upgrading your electrical panel, extending ductwork, or installing new plumbing lines.

Interior Design: Plan the interior layout, finishes, and fixtures for your addition. Consider factors like lighting, flooring, paint colors, and any built-in features you want to include. Coordinate with your contractor to ensure a smooth transition between the existing home and the new addition.

Landscaping and Exterior Integration: Once the construction is complete, consider landscaping the area around the addition to blend it with the rest of your property. This can include planting trees, installing pathways, or adding outdoor living spaces.

The penultimate chapter has also come to an end. In the final one we will talk about truly home maintenance.

Chapter 10: Home Maintenance

This chapter covers the importance of regular home maintenance tasks such as cleaning gutters, sealing gaps and cracks, and checking for water leaks. The chapter also includes a maintenance schedule to help readers stay on top of important tasks.

Regular home maintenance tasks

Regular home maintenance tasks can help keep your home in good condition and prevent major issues from arising. The most common tasks you should take into account are:

- ✓ **HVAC Maintenance:** Schedule regular inspections and servicing of your heating, ventilation, and air conditioning (HVAC) system to ensure proper functioning and energy efficiency. Replace air filters as recommended.
- ✓ **Plumbing Checks:** Regularly inspect your plumbing for leaks, drips, or other issues. Check faucets, toilets, and pipes for any signs of damage. Repair or replace any faulty fixtures.
- ✓ **Electrical System:** we have already explained. Replace or repair damaged outlets, switches, or cords. Consider hiring a professional for more complex electrical work.
- ✓ **Clean Gutters and Downspouts**
- ✓ **Roof Inspection:** control your roof for any damaged (or lacking) shingles, leaks, or other signs of wear.
- ✓ **Exterior Maintenance:** Regularly inspect the exterior of your home for cracks, peeling paint, or damaged siding. Repair or repaint as necessary to protect against moisture and maintain curb appeal.
- ✓ **Lawn and Garden Care:** keep your yard by mowing the lawn, trimming shrubs and trees, and removing weeds regularly.
- ✓ **Cleaning and Organizing:** Regularly clean your home to maintain cleanliness and prevent the buildup of dirt and allergens. Declutter and organize your living spaces to improve functionality and create a more pleasant living environment.
- ✓ **Appliance Maintenance:** Follow the manufacturer's instructions for cleaning and maintaining your appliances, such as refrigerators, ovens, dishwashers, and washing machines.
- ✓ **Safety Checks:** often control smoke detectors, carbon monoxide detectors, and fire extinguishers to be certain they are functioning. Replace batteries as needed and address any safety concerns promptly.
- ✓ Remember, this is a general list, and the specific maintenance tasks may vary depending on the age, location, and type of your home. It's always a good idea to consult manuals, hire professionals when necessary, and adapt the maintenance routine based on your specific needs.

Seasonal home maintenance tasks

Setting a home maintenance schedule can be a valid aid for you to stay organized, but also for being sure that important tasks are done in a timely manner. We are showing you below a template to help for this purpose:

Monthly

All you should do is:
- Clean or replace HVAC filters.
- Inspect and clean range hood filters.
- Check and replenish fire extinguishers.
- Clean garbage disposal.
- Look for leaks and check water pressure.
- Clean and descale faucets and showerheads.
- Test smoke detectors and carbon monoxide detectors.
- Inspect and clean dryer vents.

Seasonal

Let's see now a season schedule:

Spring
- Inspect and clean gutters and downspouts.
- Check the roof for damage and missing shingles.
- Service air conditioning system.
- Inspect and repair windows and screens.
- Trim trees and shrubs.
- Clean and repair deck or patio.

Summer
- Monitor and maintain lawn and garden.
- Inspect and clean outdoor furniture.
- Verify and change batteries in smoke detectors and carbon monoxide detectors.
- Check and clean dryer vents.

Fall
- Rake and remove leaves from the lawn.
- Clean and store outdoor furniture.
- Drain and winterize outdoor faucets and irrigation systems.
- Inspect and clean chimney and fireplace.

- ✓ Verify and adjust weather stripping.
- ✓ Have heating system serviced.

Winter
- ✓ Seal gaps and cracks in windows and doors.
- ✓ Monitor home insulation.
- ✓ Check HVAC system maintenance.
- ✓ Insulate pipes.
- ✓ Remove snow and ice from walkways and driveways.
- ✓ Verify and change batteries in smoke detectors and carbon monoxide detectors.

Annual
- ✓ Schedule a professional inspection of your heating and cooling systems.
- ✓ Hire a professional to inspect and clean the chimney.
- ✓ Conduct a home energy audit.
- ✓ Service and inspect the septic system (if applicable).
- ✓ Inspect and clean the water heater.
- ✓ Test and reset AFCIs and GFCIs throughout the house.
- ✓ Control and change weather stripping on doors and windows.
- ✓ Schedule a termite inspection.
- ✓ Deep clean carpets and upholstery.
- ✓ Clean and organize the garage.

You can also create a physical calendar, use a digital calendar app, or set reminders on your phone to ensure you stay on track with your home maintenance tasks.

Creating home maintenance schedule

Creating a home maintenance schedule is a great way to ensure that your home stays in good condition and that you address potential issues before they become major problems. Here's a step-by-step guide to help you create a comprehensive home maintenance schedule:

- ✓ **Assess your home:** Start by conducting a thorough assessment of your home, both indoors and outdoors. Identify areas that require regular maintenance or have specific needs.
- ✓ **Prioritize tasks:** Divide your maintenance tasks into categories such as seasonal, monthly, quarterly, and annual. All this can do based on tasks importance and urgency.
- ✓ **Gather information**: Research the recommended maintenance tasks for different areas of your home. Consult user manuals, manufacturer guidelines, or online resources to ensure you cover all the necessary tasks.

- ✓ **Create a calendar:** Use a physical calendar, a digital calendar, or a home maintenance app to create a schedule. Allocate specific dates or timeframes for each task, taking into account the seasonal and periodic requirements.
- ✓ **Seasonal tasks:** List tasks that need to be done during specific seasons. For example:
- ✓ **Spring:** Check and clean gutters, inspect the roof, service the HVAC system, fertilize the lawn, clean windows, etc.
- ✓ **Summer:** Inspect and maintain outdoor equipment, check for pest infestation, clean the grill, inspect and repair deck/patio, etc.
- ✓ **Fall:** Clean chimney, winterize the home, clean and store outdoor furniture, prepare the garden for winter, etc.
- ✓ **Winter:** Service the heating system, insulate pipes, clear snow and ice from walkways, check for drafts, etc.
- ✓ **Monthly and quarterly tasks:** we mean all the tasks that require to be made on a regular basis, such as:
- ✓ **Monthly:** Change HVAC filters, test smoke alarms and carbon monoxide detectors, clean range hood filters, inspect plumbing for leaks, etc.
- ✓ **Quarterly:** Deep clean carpets, test garage door safety features, clean refrigerator coils, check water softener, etc.
- ✓ **Annual tasks:** Include tasks that need to be done once a year, such as:
- ✓ Annual HVAC maintenance, including cleaning ducts and vents.
- ✓ Inspect and clean the fireplace and chimney.
- ✓ Verify and change batteries in smoke alarms and carbon monoxide detectors.
- ✓ Inspect and repair caulking and weather stripping.
- ✓ Check and clean the septic system, if applicable.
- ✓ Schedule a professional roof inspection.
- ✓ **Reminders and notifications:** Set up reminders or notifications on your calendar, smartphone, or home maintenance app to ensure you don't miss any scheduled tasks.
- ✓ **Keep a record:** Maintain a log or journal to record completed tasks, any repairs or issues discovered, and the dates of maintenance activities.
- ✓ **Adapt and adjust:** Review your home maintenance schedule periodically and make adjustments as needed. Factors like weather, age of equipment, and changes in your living situation may require modifications to the schedule.

Remember, this is a general guide, and the specific maintenance tasks may vary based on your home's age, location, and specific features. It's always a good idea to consult with professionals and follow manufacturer guidelines for specific equipment or appliances.

Hiring professionals for maintenance and repairs

Hiring professionals for maintenance and repairs can be a wise decision, especially for tasks that require specialized skills or equipment. Now, we will provide you some steps to hire professionals in a proper way:

1. Identify the specific tasks: Determine the maintenance and repair tasks that require professional assistance. This could include electrical work, plumbing repairs, HVAC servicing, roofing repairs, etc.

2. Seek recommendations: Ask friends, family, neighbors, or colleagues for recommendations of reliable professionals they have worked with in the past. Their personal experiences can help you find reputable service providers.

3. Research and gather options: Use online resources, directories, and review platforms to identify local professionals or service companies that specialize in the required tasks. Select those who get positive reviews and ratings.

4. Check qualifications and licenses: Verify that the professionals or companies you're considering are licensed, insured, and certified, if applicable to their field. This ensures they meet the necessary requirements and have the expertise to perform the job safely and effectively.

5. Request estimates: Contact a few potential professionals and ask for estimates. Provide them with clear details about the job requirements to receive accurate quotes. Be cautious of significantly low or high estimates compared to others.

6. Ask for references: Request references from the professionals or companies you're considering. Look for previous clients to ask about their experience, the quality of work, and their overall satisfaction.

7. Conduct interviews: If necessary, conduct interviews with the professionals to discuss the scope of the project, timelines, pricing, and any other relevant details.

8. Review contracts and agreements: Before hiring a professional, carefully review any contracts or agreements. Ensure that all the essential details are included, such as project scope, timelines, payment terms, and warranties or guarantees.

9. Confirm insurance coverage: Check if the professional or company has liability insurance to protect against any damages or injuries that may occur during the project.

10. Maintain open communication: Once you've hired a professional, maintain open communication throughout the project. Address any concerns or questions promptly and keep track of the progress.

Remember, hiring professionals may come at a cost, but their expertise can save you time, effort, and potential issues in the long run. By following these steps, you can increase the likelihood of finding reliable and skilled professionals for your home maintenance and repair needs.

Our complete guide to improving and repairing your home has also come to an end. We have shown you everything you need to know and what you need to make your new home unique and welcoming. What you have always wanted!

Printed in Great Britain
by Amazon